HOW TO BUILD DEVELOPER ECOSYSTEMS

From Zero to Hero: A Practical Framework for Developer-Led Growth

---

AMIR SHEVAT & MARCOS PLACONA

Contents

Preface

Why Developer Ecosystems Matter

We live in a platform economy. Amazon Web Services powers millions of businesses. Microsoft Azure and Google Cloud Platform run the infrastructure behind countless applications. Stripe processes hundreds of billions in payments. Twilio connects billions of messages and calls. Slack transformed how teams communicate. The common thread? Each built thriving developer ecosystems that created exponentially more value than the companies could generate alone.

Developer ecosystems are not just nice-to-have community programs. They are force multipliers. A single SDK, well-designed API, or open standard can ripple through startups, enterprises, and open-source communities, compounding adoption faster than any traditional marketing campaign could achieve. When developers choose your platform, they don't just use your product, they build on it, extend it, advocate for it, and bring it into their organizations.

The shift is fundamental: developers are now the decision-makers. They evaluate tools through documentation and sample code, not sales pitches. They expect self-service experiences, transparent pricing, and fast paths from "Hello World" to production. They trust peer recommendations over vendor marketing. Companies that understand this dynamic and build accordingly win market share. Those that don't struggle to gain traction, regardless of how sophisticated their technology might be.

Every technological leap, from the first web APIs to today's generative AI models, has reinforced the same pattern: platforms that win developer trust become the default choices shaping entire industries. Developer Relations has evolved from a misunderstood side function to a critical growth driver that sits at the intersection of product, marketing, community, and business strategy.

Who We Are and Why We Wrote This Book

This book draws from decades of collective experience building developer ecosystems at companies including Microsoft, Google, Slack, Twilio, Amazon, Circle, and Twitter. We've experienced the ups and downs of building developer programs, from scrappy early-stage startups to massive global platforms serving millions of developers.

We've also learned from the broader community. Throughout this book, you'll find insights from practitioners building ecosystems across different technologies, company stages, and markets. We conducted interviews with DevRel leaders, product managers, and community builders to capture diverse perspectives on what actually works. These quotes aren't inspirational fluff, they're hard-won lessons from people in the trenches.

When we began formalizing DevRel programs, most teams relied on instinct and individual heroics. Advocates carried enormous influence, but the surrounding systems were ad hoc. Companies wanted community growth but couldn't connect it to business outcomes. This book was born from frustration with that gap.

What began as internal frameworks, spreadsheets, playbooks, and dashboards evolved into the systems and approaches you'll find in these pages. Each tool was tested with real teams, measured against actual outcomes, and refined until it worked not just as theory but as practice. We've made the mistakes so you don't have to.

Amir Shevat - Amir has spent over two decades building developer ecosystems at some of the world's most influential technology companies, including Slack, Twitter, Twitch, Google, and Microsoft. He co-founded Reshuffle, a developer platform acquired by Twitter, and is currently a General Partner at Darkmode Ventures. Amir is the author of two O'Reilly books, *Designing Bots* and *Building Web APIs*

Marcos Placona - Marcos has spent over 20 years in software engineering and developer relations, building and scaling DevRel programs at companies including Twilio and Circle, where his teams won DevRel awards. He founded DevRel Bridge, a Developer Relations consultancy that helps developer-first startups drive measurable growth through strategy, content, and community

Developer Ecosystems Through the Lens of Developer Relations

Developer Relations is the role responsible for fostering developer ecosystems. While developers build on your platform, product managers define features, and marketers drive awareness, Developer Relations professionals sit at the intersection, ensuring developers can discover, adopt, and succeed with your platform.

Most of this book is written through the Developer Relations lens. Whether you're a dedicated DevRel practitioner, a founder wearing multiple hats, a product manager responsible for developer experience, or an engineer tasked with building community, you'll find the frameworks and tactics here directly applicable to your work.

A critical prerequisite: Before investing heavily in ecosystem building, ensure you have a product developers actually want to use. Product-market fit comes first. No amount of excellent documentation, vibrant community programs, or developer advocacy can compensate for a product that doesn't solve real problems or that's fundamentally difficult to use.

The most successful developer ecosystems are built on products developers genuinely love. If your API is poorly designed, your SDK is buggy, or your core value proposition is unclear, fix those issues first. Build something useful, then use the strategies in this book to help developers discover it, adopt it successfully, and build amazing things with it.

> "The reason why people built on Slack was to reach our user base. We had so many customers that developers were able to build things and reach those customers and basically generate an audience through us. Then on the

flip side, there are straight-up developer tools or infrastructure, those are products for developers that have inherent value by themselves without a user base. Stripe and Twilio are good examples."

Cecilia Stallsmith (Head of Marketing, Lovable)

Developer Relations accelerates and scales what already works. It doesn't create product-market fit where none exists.

How to Read This Book

This book is structured to be immediately actionable. Unlike traditional business books that start with definitions and philosophy, we begin with what you need to build today.

The action-first approach: We assume you're here because you want to build, not just understand theory. So we start with Chapter 1 on developer ecosystem strategy, your ICP, value proposition, and funnel. Then we give you the complete Zero to Hero framework in Chapter 2. Chapters 3-7 are pure tactics: awareness, onboarding, activation, community, and monetization. Chapter 8 shows you how to measure everything.

Then we justify and scale: Only after you understand how to build and measure do we step back in Chapter 9 to discuss what DevRel is, when to hire, organizational placement, and how to justify investment to leadership. This isn't backwards, it's practical. You need to understand what DevRel does before you can effectively argue for its value. Chapter 10 then shows you how to collaborate cross-functionally to multiply your impact.

Future-looking: Chapter 11 explores where DevRel is heading and how to stay ahead of emerging trends like AI-assisted development and agent-based onboarding.

Use the 👉 emoji: Throughout the book, you'll see chapter references marked with 👉. This makes it easy to navigate to related content when you need deeper context on a topic.

How to use this book:

- **If you're just getting started building a product or service for developers:** Read the entire book. As we say in DevRel: Read The Fantastic Manual (RTFM).
- **If you're debating whether to even start DevRel:** Read Chapter 9 first (especially "When to hire your first DevRel"), then the Preface and Chapter 1 to understand if this investment makes sense for your stage.
- **If you're launching your first DevRel hire or program:** Start with Chapter 1 (Strategy), then Chapter 2 (Framework), then dive into Chapters 3-7 in order. Skip to Chapter 9 when you need to justify headcount.
- **If you're struggling with low activation rates:** Read Chapter 4 (Onboarding) and Chapter 5 (Activation). Use the Appendix implementation sprints to fix friction points systematically.
- **If leadership is questioning DevRel's ROI:** Start with Chapter 8 (Measurement) to understand what to track, then Chapter 9 (Justification) to build your business case. Use specific metrics from Chapters 3-7 to show impact.
- **If you're scaling from 1-2 people to a full team:** Read Chapter 9 (roles and hiring), Chapter 10 (cross-functional collaboration), then revisit Chapters 3-7 to identify which functions to hire for first.

Every chapter ends with key takeaways that capture the essential points. The appendix provides tools, templates, and quick reference guides you can use immediately.

Our goal isn't to give you theory. It's to give you a playbook you can implement starting tomorrow. Whether you're a solo practitioner building your first program or leading a global DevRel team, you'll find frameworks and tactics that work.

Let's build developer ecosystems that developers actually love.

ONE

Your Developer Ecosystem Strategy

BEFORE YOU EVEN SPEAK TO DEVELOPERS, YOU NEED A STRATEGY.

Welcome to "How to Build Developer Ecosystems." This book is designed to be immediately actionable. Whether you're launching your first DevRel initiative or scaling an existing program, you'll find practical frameworks, real-world examples, and tactical guidance you can implement right away.

We're starting with strategy because it's the foundation everything else builds on. Before creating content, launching events, or building community programs, you need a clear developer ecosystem strategy. Too many companies skip this step and jump straight to tactics, which leads to wasted effort, misaligned teams, and poor results.

Your developer ecosystem strategy answers fundamental questions: Who are you building for? What value do you provide them? How will they discover, evaluate, and adopt your product? This chapter walks you through the essential components of a developer ecosystem strategy that actually works.

Define ICPs and use cases

Not all developers are created equal, and trying to serve everyone equally leads to serving no one well. Your first strategic task is defining your Ideal Customer Profile (ICP) at the developer level.

What makes a developer ICP different

Traditional B2B ICPs focus on company characteristics: industry, size, revenue, location. Developer ICPs add technical and behavioral dimensions:

Technical context: What languages, frameworks, and infrastructure do they use? Are they working in React and Node.js, or Python and Django? Do they deploy to AWS, Google Cloud, or on-premises infrastructure? These technical choices shape how they evaluate and adopt tools.

Use case specificity: What problems are they trying to solve? A developer building an e-commerce checkout experiences different pain points than one building an internal admin tool. Your ICP should capture the job to be done.

Organizational context: Are they at a startup or enterprise? Do they have procurement hurdles? Can they make decisions independently, or do they need approval? These factors affect adoption speed and patterns.

Decision authority: Who actually makes the call to adopt your tool? In some organizations, individual developers can make decisions. In others, architects, tech leads, or even procurement teams gate the decision.

Real-world ICP examples

The best ICPs are specific enough that you can visualize the individual developer, understand their constraints, and design directly for their needs. Here are three examples that demonstrate the level of specificity required:

Example 1: Rose - The Regulated Industry Technical Lead

Rose is a technical lead of a five-person engineering team at a small regional bank. She's been coding for eight years and has strong proficiency in Python and Node.js. Her current challenge is implementing a compliance workflow that requires sending text messages to phone numbers in the USA when certain regulatory thresholds are triggered.

- **Developer:** Technical lead, 8 years experience, manages small team
- **Proficiency:** Strong (Python, Node.js, comfortable with APIs)
- **Use case:** Compliance-triggered SMS notifications for banking workflows
- **Need:** Reliable SMS delivery with audit trails, US-only coverage, HIPAA/banking compliance, clear pricing per message

For Rose, your content should emphasize compliance certifications, audit capabilities, and reliability over features like international SMS or MMS. Your pricing should be transparent and predictable since she'll need to justify costs to finance. Documentation should include compliance-specific examples and integration patterns for banking systems.

Example 2: Ben - The Agency Junior Engineer

Ben is a junior engineer at a marketing agency with about two years of professional experience. He's been assigned to design a landing page for a client's product launch and needs to make it responsive, fast, and visually impressive. He's proficient in HTML/CSS and has basic JavaScript knowledge, but he's not comfortable with complex backend integrations.

- **Developer:** Junior engineer, 2 years experience, agency setting
- **Proficiency:** Moderate (HTML/CSS strong, JavaScript basics, limited backend)
- **Use case:** Build client landing pages quickly with minimal custom code
- **Need:** Pre-built templates, drag-and-drop tools, fast time-to-live, client-friendly pricing

For Ben, your Quickstart needs to get him to a working page in under 10 minutes. He needs visual examples, copy-paste code snippets, and hosted solutions that don't require infrastructure setup. Documentation should assume limited backend knowledge and focus on frontend integration. Pricing should accommodate agency models where costs pass through to clients.

Example 3: Raj - The Enterprise Data Scientist

Raj is a data scientist at MGM working on a project for a large media company. He has a PhD and strong Python skills, particularly in pandas, NumPy, and scikit-learn. He's been tasked with analyzing a massive dataset to identify sales patterns across different regions and demographics. His challenge is that the dataset is too large to process on his local machine.

- **Developer:** Data scientist, PhD-level, enterprise environment
- **Proficiency:** Expert (Python data stack, statistical analysis, limited DevOps)
- **Use case:** Distributed processing of large datasets for pattern analysis
- **Need:** Scalable compute, Python library compatibility, pay-per-use pricing, enterprise security

For Raj, documentation should show how to migrate from local pandas/NumPy code to your distributed environment with minimal changes. He needs clear guidance on data security and compliance since he's handling customer information. Your onboarding should accommodate large data uploads and provide compute scaling without requiring deep infrastructure knowledge. Pricing needs to align with his project budget cycle, not credit-card self-service.

Why this level of specificity matters

Notice how different Rose, Ben, and Raj are, and how different your DevRel approach must be for each:

- **Content depth:** Rose needs compliance whitepapers. Ben needs visual tutorials. Raj needs technical migration guides.
- **Pricing presentation:** Rose evaluates per-message costs. Ben needs client-passthrough models. Raj needs enterprise contracts.
- **Time to value:** Ben needs results in hours. Rose needs results in days with proper testing. Raj needs weeks to evaluate on production-scale data.

- **Decision process:** Ben can sign up with a credit card today. Rose needs architecture review. Raj requires procurement approval.

If you try to serve all three with the same Quickstart, the same documentation, and the same onboarding flow, you'll serve none of them well. This is why developer ICPs must go beyond generic personas to capture the technical context, proficiency level, use case, and actual needs of real developers.

The litmus test: Can you name a specific person (real or composite) who matches your ICP? If not, your ICP is too generic.

Beyond individual ICPs: While Rose, Ben, and Raj represent specific ICPs, you can also think about developers through broader behavioral archetypes. For example, Ben exhibits "Hacker" tendencies (needs quick prototypes), while Rose leans toward "Architect" concerns (reliability, compliance), and Raj combines both. These archetypes help you balance your content calendar across different developer motivations. **See Appendix A.6** for the complete Developer Archetypes framework including Hacker, Integrator, Architect, and Evangelist patterns.

Platform teams as your ICP: For infrastructure and platform products, your ICP might not be end-user developers but rather platform teams serving internal developers. These teams have unique needs, they're building on your infrastructure while simultaneously creating their own developer experience on top of it.

> "The most sophisticated customers have platform teams trying to make their internal developers' lives easier. We find ourselves in a loop: we're building infrastructure for scale and performance, and at the same time we need to provide tooling and capabilities so other platform teams can build their own onboarding systems on top of our infrastructure."
>
> Yochay Kiriaty (Director of Product Management, Google Kubernetes Engine)

Anti-personas matter too

Just as important as defining who you're targeting is defining who you're not targeting. Anti-personas help you say no to feature requests, content ideas, and partnerships that would dilute your focus.

Example anti-persona: "Hobby projects with no budget or path to production, enterprises requiring on-premise deployment with custom SLAs, developers in industries outside our compliance scope."

Anti-personas aren't about excluding people permanently. They're about focus. As you grow, you can expand to serve more segments. But initially, trying to serve everyone means serving no one well.

The ICP validation loop

Don't just guess at your ICP. Validate it with real data:

1. Interview 5-10 developers who represent your hypothesis

2. Analyze which users activate fastest and stay longest
3. Look at support tickets to identify patterns in who struggles
4. Test content and examples targeted at your ICP and measure engagement
5. Refine and iterate quarterly as you learn more

See Appendix A.5 for the complete ICP Builder Framework with templates, scoring worksheets, and validation steps.

Understanding developer motivation

Before diving into tactics, it's essential to understand what drives developers. Across languages, geographies, and seniority levels, four intrinsic motivators consistently emerge. When your DevRel programs align with these drivers, they scale naturally. When they rely on extrinsic gimmicks, they plateau.

Clarity is paramount. Developers want to quickly understand the job to be done and the shortest path to accomplish it. They don't want to wade through marketing speak or vague promises. This means you should lead with a 5-minute Quickstart that gets to the point immediately, provide runnable samples with expected output so developers know what success looks like, and make the "aha moment" obvious. If a developer can't understand what your platform does and why it matters within the first scroll, you've already lost them.

Autonomy drives adoption. Developers strongly prefer self-serve experiences over gated flows or sales calls. They want to explore, experiment, and evaluate on their own terms and time-line. In practice, this means offering instant API keys and sand-boxes without approval workflows, eliminating requirement for sales conversations just to test your product, and providing clear error messages that suggest fixes rather than leaving developers stuck. The moment you force a developer to "contact sales" or wait for manual approval, friction increases exponentially.

Progress creates momentum. Visible forward motion keeps developers engaged and building. Developers need to see that they're making headway, that their time investment is paying off. This is why displaying metrics like time-to-first-call matters, why you should add "next steps" callouts after each success to maintain momentum, and why celebrating milestones (even small ones) reinforces the developer's journey. Stagnation kills engagement faster than almost anything else.

Recognition fuels advocacy. Public artifacts and peer credibility matter deeply to developer identity. Developers build their professional reputation through their contributions, their knowledge sharing, and their visible expertise. This means you should spotlight user-generated content in your newsletters and social channels, create contributor badge programs that acknowledge different levels of participation, maintain community answer leaderboards that celebrate helpful members, and enable developers to build their reputation by associating their work with your platform. Recognition from peers often motivates continued participation more effectively than any manufactured incentive.

> "When a developer chooses to use your product, it kind of becomes part of their work identity. It's almost like you get a little logo on their jersey and they judge each other based on the products they use."
>
> Cecilia Stallsmith (Head of Marketing, Lovable)

Linking motivation to your strategy

These four drivers map directly to the stages of your developer ecosystem strategy. At the **Awareness** stage, clarity is critical. Your landing pages should communicate the "first wow" moment in seconds, not paragraphs. During **Onboarding**, autonomy takes center stage with self-service signup, instant API access, and no gatekeepers between a developer and their first API call.

As developers move into **Activation**, progress becomes the key motivator. Usage dashboards should show developers their journey from Hello World to production-ready implementation. When you reach the **Engagement** stage, recognition drives behavior through public showcases, contributor spotlights, and opportunities to co-author content with your team. Even at **Monetization**, autonomy remains important with transparent, predictable pricing that developers can evaluate independently without scheduling a call.

When you design programs around these intrinsic motivators, adoption feels natural rather than forced. Developers choose your platform because it respects how they work, not because you've gamified engagement or created artificial incentives.

Clarify your value prop for developers

Once you know who you're targeting, you need to articulate why they should care. Your developer value proposition needs to be specific, testable, and compelling.

Build versus buy decision

Every developer constantly faces this choice. Your value proposition must tip the scales toward "buy" (or "use," if you're offering a free service). The most compelling value propositions address one or more of these developer pain points:

Time to market. How much faster can developers ship their project using your solution versus building from scratch? If you can turn a three-week integration into a three-hour one, that's compelling value.

Complexity reduction. What gnarly problems do you solve that developers would rather not tackle themselves? Authentication, payment processing, and image manipulation are examples of complex domains where developers often prefer proven solutions.

Scale and reliability. What happens when their application grows? Can your solution handle the load, compliance requirements, and edge cases that they'll inevitably encounter?

Cost efficiency. Beyond the monetary cost, what's the total cost of ownership? This includes maintenance, monitoring, security updates, and the opportunity cost of engineering time spent on non-core features.

Write one sentence that pairs the job with the quantified outcome. Example: "Resize any product image in 40 minutes with one API call, no infra to manage."

Testing your value proposition

A strong value proposition should be specific enough that developers can immediately understand if it applies to them. Test yours by answering these questions:

- Can you explain the core benefit in one sentence?

- Does it address a pain point your target developers actually experience?
- Is the benefit significant enough to justify the switching cost?
- Can you prove the benefit with concrete examples or metrics?

> "We believe in the product, and we believe in the importance of developers in shaping that product to make sure it's something that they will use, want to use, and know how to use."
>
> Katie Miller (Dev Marketing Leader, former Google/Slack)

Map your developer funnel

Every developer relationship follows a predictable journey from complete stranger to successful user. Understanding this journey (your developer funnel) is crucial for designing effective programs and measuring success.

Five stages of developer adoption

We use a five-stage map throughout this book: discoverability, first win, real-world fit, belonging and growth, and value exchange. ☞ **Chapter 2** defines each stage and describes how you know you're ready to scale the next.

1. Discoverability (Awareness): The developer knows you exist and roughly understands what you do. They might have seen a tutorial, heard about you at a conference, or found you through search.

2. First win (Onboarding): The developer has successfully used your product in a trivial way. They've run Hello World or completed a basic tutorial. They know your product works, but haven't proven it solves their real problem.

3. Real-world fit (Activation): The developer has used your product to solve a real problem with real data in their context. This is the critical moment where interest transforms into genuine value.

4. Belonging and growth (Engagement): The developer returns regularly, explores additional features, participates in your community, and identifies more use cases. They're becoming a power user and advocate.

5. Value exchange (Monetization): The developer (or their company) pays for your product, or you monetize through usage, revenue sharing, or ecosystem effects. The relationship becomes financially sustainable.

Why funnel stages matter

Each stage requires different content, programs, and metrics. Awareness needs broad-reach content; activation needs specific use case guides. Conflating stages leads to mismatched efforts, for example, sending activated users to basic tutorials, or asking brand-new users to join your ambassador program.

Understanding stages also helps you identify bottlenecks. Maybe you're great at awareness but terrible at activation. Or perhaps activation is strong, but hardly anyone progresses to engagement. Knowing where developers drop off tells you where to invest effort.

Mapping content to stages

For each stage, list the content and programs that help developers progress:

Discoverability: Blog posts, tutorials, conference talks, SEO content, social media, open-source projects

First win: Quickstart guides, sample apps, getting started videos, simple SDKs

Real-world fit: Use case guides, architecture patterns, integration docs, troubleshooting guides

Belonging and growth: Community forums, office hours, beta programs, advanced tutorials, certification

Value exchange: Pricing calculators, upgrade guides, case studies, ROI documentation

How "5-min to Hello World" becomes your North Star

Among all your metrics and goals, one stands above the rest: how long does it take a developer to achieve their first successful experience with your product? This metric, often called "time to Hello World," should be your North Star.

Why speed matters

Developers are busy. They're constantly evaluating new tools, and their attention span for any single solution is limited. If they can't see value quickly, they'll move on to something else.

The Hello World moment isn't necessarily about outputting "Hello World" text. It's about the first moment when a developer thinks, "Yes, this works, and I can see how it would solve my problem" or as we call it, the "aha moment."

Designing for speed

Every decision in your developer experience should optimize for reducing the time to Hello World:

Documentation structure. Lead with the quickest path to success, not the most comprehensive explanation. Save the detailed reference material for after developers have had their first win.

API design. Prioritize simplicity in your most common use cases, even if it means more complexity in edge cases. Most developers will only explore advanced features after they've had initial success.

Authentication. Make it as easy as possible to get started. Consider offering API keys that work immediately without requiring email verification or complex OAuth flows.

Sample code. Provide working examples that developers can copy, paste, and run immediately. Nothing builds confidence like seeing immediate results.

> *"You should optimize for the time-to-aha moment. The onboarding flow is not about time to production , it's about showing the power as fast as possible. Get developers to that first success, then build on top of that."*
>
> Zeno Rocha (Co-founder & CEO, Resend)

Measuring time to Hello World

Track this metric religiously:

- Time from signup to first API call
- Time from first documentation visit to successful implementation
- Support ticket volume in the first 24 hours after signup
- Percentage of developers who achieve first success within your target timeframe

Note: Not all Hello Word look the same, your product might be more complex than others. For example, your API might require installing dedicated hardware or additional software.

> "In Hardware, the time to Hello World is so much longer because, you don't know: do they have the right device? Are they on Windows or Mac? Doing a hardware-focused developer training is very complex."
>
> Jonathan Beri (Founder, Golioth; ex-Google IoT)

Measuring funnel performance

Your developer ecosystem strategy isn't complete without a clear plan for measuring performance. Different metrics matter at different stages, and tracking the wrong things can lead you astray.

Leading versus lagging indicators

Leading indicators tell you what's happening now and predict future outcomes. Examples include documentation CTR, quickstart completion rate, and community response times. These metrics let you course-correct quickly.

Lagging indicators tell you what already happened and validate long-term success. Examples include activated users, seven-day retention, and revenue. These metrics are important for proving ROI but arrive too late to guide day-to-day decisions.

You need both. Leading indicators guide your tactics; lagging indicators prove your strategy is working.

Stage-specific metrics

Each funnel stage needs its own metrics:

Discoverability: Tutorial to quickstart CTR, branded search volume, qualified traffic growth **First win:** Quickstart completion rate, median time to first call, first-call success rate **Real-world fit:** Activation rate, seven-day retention, production key creation rate **Belonging and growth:** Community answer rate, feature breadth per account, user-generated content **Value exchange:** Trial to paid conversion, expansion revenue, net retention rate

We'll dive deeper into metrics and measurement in ☞ **Chapter 8**.

Avoid vanity metrics

Not all metrics are created equal. Vanity metrics look impressive but don't predict business outcomes:

Social media followers matter less than community engagement and conversion **Total documentation views** matter less than completion rates and success metrics **Event attendance** matters less than post-event activation and engagement **Total GitHub stars** matter less than active usage and contributions

Focus on metrics that tie directly to developer success and business outcomes.

Bring user feedback back to the product group

Your developer ecosystem strategy isn't complete without a clear process for turning developer feedback into product improvements. DevRel sits at a unique vantage point: they hear directly from developers while understanding product strategy. This position makes them invaluable for product improvement, but only if feedback loops actually work.

> "Showing a developer or product person a video of someone saying 'my god, this is utter rubbish' and they are the person who built it, that strikes emotion. Show the statistical numbers: nothing happens. Show five videos of people swearing at your product: instantly, things get fixed."
>
> Jim Bennett (Principal Developer Experience Engineer, Arize AI)

Structured feedback collection

Support channels. Every support interaction is a learning opportunity. Create systems to tag, categorize, and analyze support tickets to identify patterns.

Community conversations. Forums, Discord channels, and social media contain valuable unstructured feedback. Regular reviews of these conversations surface issues docs and FAQs should address.

User interviews. Regular conversations with users at different stages of adoption reveal pain points and opportunities that metrics alone can't capture.

Beta programs. Early access programs provide concentrated feedback on new features before they affect your entire user base. We'll cover beta programs in detail in ☛ **Chapter 6**.

Making feedback actionable

Raw feedback isn't enough. DevRel needs to:

1. Identify patterns and themes across multiple feedback sources
2. Prioritize issues by frequency and impact
3. Document specific examples and reproduction steps
4. Propose solutions or alternatives when possible
5. Present feedback in language product teams understand

Closing the loop

Tell developers what happened with their feedback. When you make changes based on community input, announce it. When you can't implement a request, explain why. This transparency builds trust and encourages continued feedback.

See ☛ **Chapter 10** for detailed guidance on cross-functional collaboration and feedback loops with product teams.

Key takeaways

Strategy before tactics. Don't create content or programs until you know who you're targeting, what value you provide, and how developers move through your funnel.

ICP focus drives results. Define your ideal developer profile with technical, behavioral, and organizational dimensions. Create anti-personas to maintain focus.

Value propositions must be specific. Generic claims don't convince developers. Quantify the time saved, complexity reduced, or problems solved.

Map your complete funnel. Understand the five stages from discoverability to value exchange. Different stages need different content and metrics.

Speed to first success matters most. Optimize relentlessly for reducing time to Hello World. This metric predicts everything downstream.

Feedback loops are mandatory. Create structured processes to collect, analyze, and act on developer feedback. Close the loop by telling developers what changed.

With your strategy clear, you're ready to understand the complete DevRel framework in **Chapter 2**, where we'll map specific programs and activities to each stage of the developer journey.

TWO

The Zero to Hero Framework

OPTIMIZING THE DEVELOPER JOURNEY. THE FIVE STAGES EVERY DEVELOPER GOES THROUGH, MAPPED TO DEVREL ACTIVITIES.

The five-stage framework

Understanding that developers move through stages is one thing. Knowing exactly what to do at each stage is another. This chapter provides a comprehensive framework that maps specific DevRel activities, content types, metrics, and programs to each stage of the developer journey.

Think of this as your DevRel playbook. We'll define what "green" looks like for each stage, identify common bottlenecks, and provide stage gates that tell you when you're ready to scale to the next level.

Stage 1: Awareness (Discoverability)

Promise: I know this tool exists and vaguely understand its superpower.

Primary goal: Get on the radar of the right developers with the right message.

Not about: Reaching everyone or maximizing impressions. It's about reaching developers who have the problem you solve.

Example key activities:

- Build an SEO-optimized developer destination with tutorials and blog posts
- Deliver conference talks and presentations
- Create open-source projects and contribute to existing ones
- Participate in developer communities
- Maintain online advocacy and social media presence (LinkedIn, Twitter/X, etc.)
- Build partner and integrator relationships
- Publish documentation as content
- Create video tutorials and demos

Note: The specific activities that work best will vary depending on your platform, target audience, available budget, and team skills. These examples represent common high-impact activities, but you should adapt based on your constraints and context.

Critical success factors:

- Message discipline: one sentence that pairs problem with promise

- Fast path to activation: every awareness asset links to quickstart
- Right audience, not maximum audience
- UTM tracking on all external content

Metrics to track:

- Leading: Tutorial to quickstart CTR, qualified traffic sources
- Lagging: Branded search volume, time-delayed conversions

Stage gate: Proceed to Stage 2 only when awareness is converting to signups from quality sources, not just driving traffic.

👉 **See Chapter 3** for detailed tactics on building awareness that converts.

Stage 2: Onboarding (First Win)

Promise: I can get this working in minutes, and I understand the basics.

Primary goal: Convert curiosity into confidence through a fast, friction-free first success.

Not about: Comprehensive education or advanced features. It's about proving it works quickly.

Example key activities:

- Create quickstart guides optimized for speed
- Provide interactive sandboxes and hosted environments
- Build sample applications with one-click deploy
- Design clear, simple authentication flows
- Provide working code snippets for common scenarios
- Create video walkthroughs of setup process

Critical success factors:

- Time to first call under 5 minutes
- One clear path, not multiple options
- Immediate visible results
- Clear next steps after Hello World

Metrics to track:

- Leading: Quickstart completion rate, setup drop-off points
- Lagging: Median time to first call, first-call success rate

Stage gate: Don't scale awareness campaigns until median time to first call is under 5 minutes and first-call success rate exceeds 80%.

☞ **See Chapter 4** for detailed tactics on creating friction-free onboarding experiences.

Stage 3: Activation (Real-World Fit)

Promise: This solves my actual problem with my actual data in my actual workflow.

Primary goal: Help developers transition from toy examples to production use.

Not about: Just making more API calls. It's about meaningful usage that delivers real value.

Example key activities:

- Create use-case-driven documentation
- Publish integration guides for popular tools and frameworks
- Document architecture patterns and best practices
- Provide production deployment checklists
- Write troubleshooting guides for common issues
- Develop performance and optimization resources
- Document error handling and retry patterns

Critical success factors:

- Clear activation milestone definition
- Content that bridges demo to production
- Observability and debugging support
- Production-ready code examples

Metrics to track:

- Leading: Percentage hitting activation milestone within 24 hours

- Lagging: Seven-day activation retention, production key creation rate

Stage gate: Don't build community programs until activation rate exceeds 20% and production usage is measurable.

👉 **See Chapter 5** for detailed tactics on driving developer activation beyond Hello World.

Stage 4: Engagement (Belonging and Growth)

Promise: I'm part of a community that helps me succeed and grow with this platform.

Primary goal: Transform activated users into an engaged community that supports itself.

Not about: One-way communication or vendor-controlled spaces. It's about peer connections and shared learning.

Example key activities:

- Host community forums and Discord servers
- Run regular office hours and live Q&A
- Launch champion and ambassador programs
- Operate beta testing and early access programs
- Organize hackathons and coding challenges
- Facilitate user-generated content and showcases
- Implement contributor recognition programs

Critical success factors:

- Peer-to-peer support exceeding staff support
- Community answering questions in under 24 hours
- Regular user-generated content
- Clear paths from participant to contributor to champion

Metrics to track:

- Leading: Community answer rate, peer response time
- Lagging: Feature breadth per account, user-generated content per month

Stage gate: Don't launch monetization campaigns until community answer rate exceeds 65% and engagement is self-sustaining.

☞ **See Chapter 6** for detailed tactics on building engaged, self-sustaining developer communities.

Stage 5: Monetization (Value Exchange)

Promise: Paying gives me additional value, and I feel good about it.

Primary goal: Convert usage and trust into sustainable revenue without breaking the developer relationship.

Not about: Aggressive sales tactics or artificial paywalls. It's about aligning payment with value delivery.

Example key activities:

- Create clear pricing page, calculators and cost estimators if needed
- Publish "when to upgrade" documentation
- Develop usage optimization guides
- Create ROI and case study content
- Provide enterprise feature education
- Enable sales without DevRel carrying quotas
- Showcase customer success stories

Critical success factors:

- Transparent, predictable pricing
- DevRel promotes healthy usage, not sales
- Clear handoff to sales for enterprise deals
- Upgrade triggers based on value delivery

Metrics to track:

- Leading: Pricing page views by activated users, upgrade intent signals

- Lagging: Trial to paid conversion, expansion revenue, net retention

Stage gate: Monetization is healthy when it deepens trust rather than replaces it.

👉 **See Chapter 7** for detailed tactics on driving value exchange and sustainable monetization.

Cross-stage principles

Certain principles apply across all stages:

Developer empathy above all. Every program, piece of content, and metric should start with understanding the developer's context, constraints, and goals.

Measurement drives improvement. Each stage needs both leading indicators (what to fix now) and lagging indicators (proof it's working).

Stage discipline prevents chaos. Don't skip stages or scale the next stage before the current one is healthy. Awareness without onboarding wastes budget. Community without activation wastes goodwill.

Feedback loops are mandatory. Every stage should have mechanisms to capture what's working and what's not, then close the loop with improvements and communication.

Common anti-patterns to avoid

Hero syndrome. One charismatic advocate creates a single point of failure. Build systems and teams, not dependencies on individuals.

Vanity metrics. Optimizing for followers, stars, or event attendance instead of activation and retention leads you astray.

Stage skipping. Launching ambassador programs before you have activation, or scaling awareness before onboarding works, wastes resources and damages trust.

Random acts of advocacy. Doing activities because they

seem like "DevRel things" rather than because they advance specific stage goals dilutes impact.

Feedback blackhole. Collecting developer input but never acting on it teaches developers their voice doesn't matter.

Framework flexibility

While this five-stage framework covers the most common developer journey for platforms that monetize, your platform may be different. Some platforms never pursue monetization. Slack famously built one of the strongest developer ecosystems without charging developers directly. Others might combine or skip stages based on their business model.

Feel free to adapt this framework to your specific use case. If you're building an open-source project, you might emphasize community engagement over monetization. If you're in enterprise sales, activation might look very different than described here. The principles of progressive engagement, stage gates, and measurement remain valuable even when the specific stages differ.

Use this framework as a starting point, not a rigid prescription. Map your own journey if your platform has unique characteristics that don't fit the standard pattern.

Key takeaways

Five stages map the complete journey. From awareness through monetization, each stage needs specific activities, content, and metrics.

Stage gates prevent premature scaling. Don't advance to the next stage until the current one is healthy. Awareness without working onboarding wastes money.

Leading and lagging metrics together. Leading indicators guide daily decisions; lagging indicators prove long-term success.

Systems beat heroes. Sustainable programs outlive charismatic individuals. Build repeatable processes and clear ownership.

Maturity takes time. Plan for the long term. DevRel impact compounds over quarters and years, not days and weeks.

Now that you understand the framework, let's dive into Stage 1 in ☞ **Chapter 3**, where we'll explore exactly how to build awareness that actually converts.

THREE

Awareness: Make Developers Care

IT'S NOT ABOUT SHOUTING LOUDER, IT'S ABOUT BEING IN THE RIGHT PLACES WITH THE RIGHT MESSAGE.

You've built an incredible product. Your team has crafted elegant endpoints, your documentation is comprehensive, and your value proposition is crystal clear. But here's the harsh reality: none of that matters if developers don't know you exist. In the noisy world of developer tools and platforms, awareness isn't just the first step in your developer funnel. It's the foundation everything else is built on.

The "if you build it, they will come" mentality is one of the most dangerous misconceptions in developer relations. Every day, brilliant APIs launch into obscurity because their creators assumed technical excellence would naturally lead to adoption. It won't. Even the most established platforms like Stripe, Twilio, and AWS invest heavily in awareness campaigns because they understand a fundamental truth: in a world where new developer tools launch daily, staying visible is an ongoing battle, not a one-time victory.

The awareness paradox

Effective developer awareness is fundamentally different from traditional marketing. Developers are skeptical of marketing messages, allergic to hype, and quick to dismiss anything that feels like a sales pitch. Yet they need to discover new tools somehow. This paradox shapes everything about developer awareness:

Developers want solutions, not sales pitches. When a developer searches for "how to process payments in Node.js," they're not looking for product comparisons. They want a tutorial that solves their immediate problem. The companies that win awareness are those that provide genuine value upfront.

Trust comes from peers, not vendors. A recommendation from another developer carries far more weight than any marketing campaign. This makes community presence, content quality, and authentic relationships far more valuable than paid advertising.

Technical depth matters. Surface-level content gets ignored. Developers respect companies that demonstrate real expertise and understanding of their challenges.

Understanding your developer audience

Before you can build effective awareness, you need to understand who you're trying to reach and where they are. This goes beyond the ICP work from **Chapter 1**. You need to understand how different types of developers discover and evaluate new tools.

Developers aren't a monolithic group. A solo developer building a side project evaluates tools differently than an enterprise architect selecting platforms for a team of 50. A frontend engineer has different needs and discovery patterns than a backend engineer or DevOps specialist.

Discovery patterns by developer type

Hobbyist developers discover via social media, YouTube, Reddit, and side projects. They're motivated by fun, learning, and fast starts. Your message: "What can I build in an hour?"

Professional developers discover via colleagues, Stack Overflow, vendor docs, and technical blogs. They're motivated by reliability, integrations, and time saved. Your message: "Ship faster with proven tools."

Enterprise developers discover via architecture reviews, vendor lists, peer recommendations at conferences, and security/compliance requirements. They're motivated by security, compliance, support, and procurement-readiness. Your message: "Enterprise-grade with support."

> "You're going to need to gauge and get really clear on what is your target audience and how technical are they and what languages, what do they speak? You want to speak in their language."
>
> Cecilia Stallsmith (Head of Marketing, Lovable)

One size doesn't fit all. Your awareness strategy should include multiple channels and message variants that speak to these different personas in their native contexts.

Message discipline rule: Create one sentence that pairs the problem with the promise, and repeat it consistently across all your awareness channels: landing pages, conference talks, documentation, social media, and community posts. This consistency helps developers quickly recognize and remember your value proposition regardless of where they encounter you.

Content as the foundation

Content is the cornerstone of developer awareness, but not all content is created equal. The most effective awareness content doesn't just inform. It inspires, educates, and demonstrates value simultaneously. Think of your content as a gateway for your API: it should give developers a taste of what's possible and leave them wanting more.

Landing pages that work

Your developer landing page is often the first impression developers have of your API. It's also one of the most underutilized awareness assets. Most developer landing pages fail because they're designed like traditional marketing pages: heavy on benefits, light on specifics, and missing the quick path to actual code.

What works on developer landing pages:

Immediate clarity. Within five seconds of landing, a developer should understand what you do and for whom. Use one clear headline that states the problem you solve and the technology context.

Show, don't just tell. Include a code snippet right on the homepage. Even better, make it interactive so developers can modify and run it without signing up.

Fast path to Hello World. The primary CTA should link directly to your quickstart guide, not a general "get started" page. Every second counts.

Social proof that matters. Generic "trusted by 10,000 companies" claims don't resonate. Instead, show logos developers recognize, GitHub stats that demonstrate activity, and specific use cases from companies similar to your target audience.

Technical credibility signals. Link to your documentation, GitHub repo, and API reference. Show your tech stack compatibility, supported languages, and framework integrations.

> "SDKs, documentation, and example projects are critical. When you're connecting hardware and cloud software, good docs become even more important because there are more places things can break."
>
> Jonathan Beri (Founder, Golioth; ex-Google IoT)

Docs as content, not just support

Documentation serves dual purposes: it helps existing users use your product better, and it attracts new users through search and sharing. Too many companies treat docs as purely support material, missing the massive awareness opportunity.

Documentation that drives awareness:

SEO-optimized from the start. Every doc page should target specific searches developers make. Use real queries as H1s ("How to send SMS in Python" not "Python SDK").

Answer-first structure. Put the working code example at the top, explanation below. Developers want solutions first, understanding second.

Version stamps and freshness. Date your docs and mark compatibility explicitly. Nothing kills trust like finding outdated documentation.

Searchable and linkable. Every section needs a permanent, hackable URL. Developers share specific solutions, not homepage links.

Progressive disclosure. Use collapsible sections, tabs, and clear hierarchy so beginners and experts can both find what they need quickly.

Blogs, tutorials, and SEO

Written content remains one of the most effective awareness channels for developer products, but here's the thing: format matters tremendously. Not all developer content performs equally.

Tutorial-driven content strategy

If you're going to invest in content, tutorials should be your first priority. They outperform thought leadership pieces 10:1 for developer awareness. Why such a dramatic difference? Tutorials solve immediate problems while simultaneously demonstrating your product's value. Developers don't come to your site for philosophical musings about the future of APIs, they come because they're stuck on something right now, and they need it fixed.

Great developer tutorials share a few key characteristics. First, they're specific. "Building a real-time chat app with WebSockets and your API" beats "Intro to WebSockets" every single time because developers search for solutions to specific problems, not general education. Second, the code actually works. GitHub repos that clone and run in under 30 seconds get shared and bookmarked. Complex setups that require an hour of environment configuration get abandoned before they're even started.

Your tutorials should also show production-ready patterns, not toy examples. Include error handling, retries, and logging. Developers can tell the difference between demo code and code they could actually deploy, and they respect companies that show them the real deal. This is where you build trust.

Pay attention to your titles too. Use the actual searches developers make. Tools like Google Keyword Planner or AnswerThePublic reveal search patterns, but honestly, your own support tickets are probably the best source. If five developers asked the same question this month, hundreds more are searching for it. Finally, remember that developers have different learning styles. Some prefer reading step-by-step instructions, others want to watch someone do it. When you can, do both, a 5-minute video plus written steps plus a working code repo covers all the bases.

SEO fundamentals for developer content

Developer SEO has some unique characteristics that distinguish it from traditional B2B SEO. For one thing, code snippets aren't just illustrations, they're actual content. Search engines can't execute your code, but they recognize it. Well-commented code with clear variable names actually helps your SEO.

Look at Stack Overflow questions as a keyword goldmine. If developers are asking a question there, they're definitely searching for it on Google. Pay attention to how they phrase things. Developers also search with precision, so version-specific content matters. Don't just target "React", target "React 18" or "Python 3.12" explicitly.

Here's an insight that surprises many content teams: you should target the problem state as much as the solution state. Developers often search for error messages verbatim, like "TypeError: 'NoneType' object is not iterable." If your content answers that specific error in context of your platform, you'll capture those searches.

Finally, technical depth demonstrates expertise in ways that shallow content never can. Don't be afraid to go deep. Show that you understand edge cases, performance implications, and architectural trade-offs. Thin content gets ignored by developers who can spot surface-level understanding from a mile away.

Events, videos, and open source

While written content forms the foundation, other channels multiply your reach and build different types of credibility.

"You have to play to your strengths. Shawn "Swyx" Wang does writing really well. I'm very bad at writing, so I don't focus on that. What I'm good at is organizing people in real life settings, conferences, meetups, drink ups. That's how I interact with developers."

Ivan Burazin (Founder, Daytona)

Conference presence that converts

Conference talks offer high-impact awareness opportunities, but most companies waste them by treating conferences as sales opportunities rather than education and networking events. Here's what actually works.

Getting your team speaking should be priority one. A 25-minute technical talk reaches and impacts developers far more than a booth with swag ever will. But that talk needs to deliver value beyond pitching your product. Share knowledge freely and teach something genuinely useful even if someone never uses your product. Give before you take.

Demo quality can make or break your credibility. A glitchy demo kills trust instantly, so practice until your demos are bulletproof. Have backup plans and offline fallbacks ready. When things go smoothly, you look competent. When they don't, you look unprepared.

Make it easy for interested developers to take the next step. Every slide deck should end with a direct link, ideally via QR code, to your quickstart guide rather than your homepage. And don't let the value of that talk end when the session does. Turn it into a blog post, a YouTube video, a GitHub repo, and social posts.

One 25-minute talk should generate ten pieces of content that continue working for you long after the conference ends.

Video content strategy

Video has become increasingly important for developer awareness, but it requires different thinking than traditional video marketing. Developers want substance over production value, and the most effective videos reflect that priority.

Quickstart walkthroughs work best at 3-5 minutes. These are simple screen recordings showing the exact steps from zero to working code. You don't need fancy production, just clear audio and visible code. Similarly, problem-solution demos (5-10 minutes) should show a real problem and then solve it with your tool, ideally comparing it to the alternative approach so developers can see the difference.

When you want to go deeper, architecture explainers (10-15 minutes) let you explain how something works internally. Developers respect companies that explain their technical decisions openly. And don't forget that your conference talks can have a second life. Professional recording and editing of your best talks extend their reach far beyond the event itself.

One of the most effective formats is often the simplest: let your users explain how they use your product. Developer interviews and user stories carry authenticity that beats polish every time.

Open source as awareness

Open source is paradoxically both the most natural and most misunderstood developer awareness channel. Done well, it builds tremendous credibility. Done poorly, it damages your reputation.

Start with utility, not promotion. Create genuinely useful tools that happen to work well with your platform but don't require it. The most successful developer tools solve frustrations even if they're small. A great CLI, a helpful linter, or elegant error messages builds goodwill in ways that promotional repos never will.

Consistent maintenance matters more than your initial release. An abandoned repo is worse than no repo at all because it signals that your company starts things it doesn't finish. Commit to responding to issues and reviewing PRs within 48 hours. This consistency builds trust.

Beyond your own projects, contributing to popular projects that your developers use builds credibility and exposes your team to new audiences. These contributions show that you're part of the developer community, not just marketing to it.

A note on scope: This section focuses on open source as an awareness strategy, releasing useful tools and contributing to the ecosystem to build credibility. If you're running an open-core business model where open source is fundamental to your product strategy, that's a different conversation entirely. We're talking about tactical open source initiatives that raise awareness, not business models built on open source foundations.

Distribution: dev communities, partner channels

Creating great content is only half the battle. You need distribution channels that reach developers where they already are.

Developer community presence

Developers congregate in specific online spaces, and each has its own culture and expectations. Understanding where to show up and how to behave makes the difference between building credibility and getting ignored or downvoted into oblivion.

GitHub is more than just a place to host your code. It's a social network for developers. Meaningful participation builds awareness organically. Leave helpful comments on issues in related projects, submit quality pull requests, and engage authentically with the community. This kind of presence compounds over time.

Stack Overflow rewards expertise and helpfulness. Answer questions related to your domain honestly and helpfully, even when the answer doesn't involve your product. Your goal is to build a reputation first, not to promote. When you consistently provide value, people notice and start trusting your technical judgment.

Reddit communities like r/programming, r/webdev, and technology-specific subreddits welcome genuinely helpful content but have zero tolerance for anything that smells promotional. These communities instantly downvote self-promotion. Show up to help, not to market.

Similarly, Discord and Slack communities are where developers hang out and help each other. Join communities where your target developers spend time. Be helpful. Don't promote. The moment you start pushing your product, you've lost the room.

Twitter/X remains relevant for developer audiences, especially for sharing quick tips, asking questions, and engaging with other developers and DevRel folks. It's a good place for building relationships and staying connected to the broader developer community.

Cross-posting your content to platforms like Dev.to, Hashnode, and Medium can extend your reach significantly. Developers already read there, so meet them where they are. Just make sure your content is genuinely useful, not thinly veiled marketing.

The golden rule: Give 10x more value than you take. Help freely, promote sparingly.

A note on the shifting landscape: Developer communities and presence strategies are constantly evolving. At the time of this writing, Stack Overflow is losing momentum as developers increasingly turn to AI solutions for answers. The platforms that matter today may not be the platforms that matter tomorrow. We'll explore how to optimize for AI-powered search and discovery in Chapter 11 on the future of Developer Relations.

Partner and integrator relationships

Strategic partnerships can dramatically amplify your awareness efforts by putting you in front of relevant developer audiences you haven't reached yet. The key is finding partners whose audiences overlap with yours but who aren't competing for the same developer mindshare.

Framework and library integrations give you visibility in established ecosystems. Building official plugins or examples for popular frameworks like React, Vue, Django, or Rails puts your tool in front of developers who are already committed to those technologies and looking for solutions that integrate well.

Platform marketplace listings provide built-in distribution. Shopify, WordPress, Salesforce, and other platforms with app marketplaces have millions of developers browsing for tools. Getting listed in these marketplaces can drive significant awareness with minimal additional effort.

Technology partnerships with complementary (not competing) developer tools let you reach relevant audiences efficiently. Co-marketing arrangements work well when both companies benefit from the association and serve similar but non-overlapping needs.

Developer program partnerships through GitHub Education, AWS Activate, Google for Startups, and similar programs provide both credibility and distribution. These programs attract developers who are actively building new projects and looking for tools to use.

Community partnerships around sponsoring meetups, hackathons, or community events in your technical domain build local awareness and credibility. These partnerships show that you're investing in the developer community, not just extracting value from it.

Measuring awareness impact

Awareness is notoriously difficult to measure directly, but several metrics help you understand your impact.

Track paired metrics for each awareness stream:

Content to quickstart:

- Leading: Tutorial to quickstart CTR
- Lagging: First successful API calls attributed to that tutorial's UTM

Docs SEO:

- Leading: Organic clicks to solution pages
- Lagging: Percentage of those sessions that run the quickstart within the same session

Social:

- Leading: Click-through to quickstart from posts
- Lagging: First calls within 24 hours of the click

Events/talks:

- Leading: QR scans to quickstart
- Lagging: First calls within 24 hours of the scan

Partners/marketplaces:

- Leading: Referral clicks to quickstart
- Lagging: First calls in the first session after referral

Establish baselines, review week over week, and move from awareness to onboarding optimization when both the leading and lagging pairs trend up for at least two consecutive reviews. (Refer back to Chapter 2's framework: don't scale to the next stage until the current one is healthy.)

> "It took us six months from when we started to when we were getting people coming in. All those steps take time. On average, the six month period is when you start feeling if it's working or not."
>
> Ivan Burazin (Founder, Daytona)

The long game of developer awareness

Building developer awareness is fundamentally different from traditional marketing. It's not about campaigns or launches but about consistently providing value, building relationships, and earning trust over time. The most successful developer awareness strategies feel less like marketing and more like education, community building, and genuine contribution to the developer ecosystem.

> "Trust is consistency over time."
>
> Cecilia Stallsmith (Head of Marketing, Lovable)

Awareness isn't a destination but a continuous journey. Even the most well-known APIs must constantly work to maintain their visibility in an increasingly crowded marketplace. The winning companies are those that view awareness as an ongoing investment in their developer community rather than a one-time marketing challenge.

Key takeaways

Targeted awareness fuels efficient onboarding. Right eyes, not all eyes. Focus on ICP developers who feel the pain your product fixes.

Content demonstrates value, not just features. Tutorials, working code, and problem-solving content outperform feature lists and benefits statements.

SEO is your force multiplier. Developer-focused SEO targets specific problems, version-specific searches, and technical depth. It compounds over time.

Distribution beats creation alone. Great content needs distribution. Meet developers where they are in communities, events, and partner ecosystems.

Trust comes from peers and proof. Social proof that matters to developers: GitHub activity, technical depth in content, and authentic community presence.

Every awareness asset must link to quickstart. Never send developers to a generic homepage. Fast path to activation is non-negotiable.

Measure what matters, pair leading and lagging. Tutorial CTR predicts activation. Branded search confirms awareness is sticking.

In **Chapter 4**, we'll explore how to convert that hard-earned awareness into successful onboarding experiences that turn interested developers into active users of your API.

FOUR

Onboarding: First Impressions Count

YOU HAVE ONE SHOT. DON'T WASTE IT.

The moment a developer discovers your product is magical, but also fleeting. Within minutes, sometimes seconds, they'll decide whether your platform is worth their time or if they should move on to a competitor. This critical window is your onboarding experience, and it can make or break your entire developer ecosystem.

> "If your five-minute hello world leaves developers stuck afterward, that's not helpful. The aha moment is when developers actually get value, not just when they see an example."
>
> Katie Miller (Dev Marketing Leader, former Google/Slack)

You spent months building awareness through content, events, and community participation. A developer finally arrives at your documentation, curious and ready to try your product. What happens in the next five minutes determines whether they become an active user or just another statistic in your drop-off metrics.

The five-minute window

Research across thousands of developer onboarding experiences reveals a harsh truth: if developers can't see value within five minutes, most will abandon your product entirely. This isn't because developers are impatient or your product is bad. It's because developers face an overwhelming number of choices, constant time pressure, and countless distractions competing for their attention.

The five-minute window isn't arbitrary. It represents the average amount of focused time a developer will invest in evaluating a new tool before deciding whether to continue or move on. Within those five minutes, they're forming judgments about:

Does this actually solve my problem? Abstract descriptions don't convince. Working code does.

Can I trust this company? Poor documentation, broken examples, or confusing errors signal potential problems ahead.

Is this worth my time? Friction in setup, unclear next steps, or missing information all increase the perceived cost of adoption.

Will I be stuck if I commit? Developers worry about vendor lock-in, missing features, and what happens when things go wrong.

Your onboarding experience must address all these concerns quickly and convincingly.

> "It doesn't matter how good the product is, if developers can't get started with it, they're not going to use it. Developers have a very short attention span, and there are so many products out there. The trick is defining what the wow moment is, and then working out the simplest journey to get there."
>
> Jim Bennett (Principal Developer Experience Engineer, Arize AI)

Dev portals and getting started guides

Your developer portal is more than just a documentation site. It's the first real interaction developers have with your product, and it sets expectations for everything that follows.

> "You as a marketer often aren't thinking about docs as a channel, but as a developer marketer, docs are one of your number one channels and I would be making sure those are amazing."

Cecilia Stallsmith (Head of Marketing, Lovable)

The anatomy of effective developer portals

Developers should find what they need without searching. This sounds obvious, but most developer portals fail at basic information architecture. Three top-level sections work for most APIs: Getting Started, API Reference, and Guides/Tutorials. Clear, simple, predictable.

Above the fold, answer three questions immediately: What do you do? Who is this for? How fast can they get started? Use one clear sentence. Developers shouldn't have to scroll or click to understand if they're in the right place.

Use progressive disclosure to guide developers through complexity. Show the quick path prominently and hide the advanced stuff until it's needed. Your portal should feel like a funnel, not a maze. The visual hierarchy should naturally guide developers from awareness to action.

Developers search more than browse. Invest in search quality and make sure it includes code samples and error messages in results. Nothing is more frustrating than knowing the answer exists somewhere in your docs but not being able to find it.

Version awareness matters. Nothing breaks trust faster than documentation that doesn't match the product version developers are actually using. Mark versions clearly and maintain docs for at least two major versions back. Developers work with legacy systems and can't always upgrade on your schedule.

Getting started guides that convert

Your getting started guide is the most important page in your entire documentation. It's where awareness converts to activation or dies. Developers land here with intent, they want to try your product. Your job is to make that as frictionless as possible.

Don't offer five different ways to get started. Pick the fastest path for your primary ICP and optimize that ruthlessly. **One clear path** beats multiple mediocre options every time. You can add alternative approaches later, but the default path should be obvious.

List prerequisites upfront before developers invest time. Nothing frustrates more than discovering ten minutes in that you need Python 3.9 but only have 3.7 installed. Respect developers' time by being transparent about requirements from the start.

Show the complete, working example in the first 30 seconds. Working code first, explanation after success. This is counterintuitive for many technical writers who want to explain concepts first, but developers learn by doing. They want to see it work, then understand why.

Make everything copy-paste friendly. Developers should be able to copy and run your examples with zero modifications. Use hard-coded API keys for testing, include sample data, provide everything needed to succeed immediately. Remove every possible point of friction.

Show exactly what success looks like. Include screenshots, logs, terminal output, whatever confirms "it worked." Developers need to know they're on the right track. Without clear expected output, they'll second-guess whether they did it correctly.

After Hello World, give developers a clear next step. Don't leave them hanging with "Congratulations, it works!" The momentum from that initial success is powerful. Channel it immediately into the next logical action, whether that's exploring use cases, customizing the example, or deploying to production.

Auth and setup patterns

Authentication is often the biggest friction point in developer onboarding. It's necessary for security but can feel like an obstacle when developers just want to try your product.

The authentication trade-off

Security requirements often conflict with ease of use. The best developer experiences find ways to make authentication feel natural rather than burdensome.

The ideal approach is to let developers try your API without even creating an account. Provide a test key right in the docs that works for sample requests. This removes the biggest barrier to that crucial first API call. Developers can see your product work before committing to anything.

When possible, delay account creation until developers actually need it. Let them experiment with your product first, then create an account only when they want to save their work or move to production. This respects the natural flow of evaluation: try it, like it, commit to it.

Start with the simplest authentication that works. Save OAuth, JWT, and complex auth patterns for production use. Simple key-based auth gets developers started fast. You can always guide them toward more sophisticated auth methods once they've decided your product is worth integrating properly.

Provide a clear sandbox environment where developers can experiment without worrying about costs, rate limits, or breaking things. Fear kills experimentation. A safe playground where mistakes don't matter encourages developers to explore your full feature set.

Show rate limits and quotas clearly. Surprises during evaluation kill adoption. Developers need to know what they're working with, especially if they're evaluating whether your platform can handle their production scale. Hidden limits that suddenly appear feel like bait-and-switch, even when they're reasonable.

Common auth patterns and when to use them

API keys: Best for getting started and simple integrations. Easy to understand and implement. Risk: can be accidentally committed to public repos.

OAuth 2.0: Necessary for user-level permissions and third-party integrations. More complex but standard across the industry. Save for production scenarios.

JWTs: Good for stateless auth. Modern libraries and services make JWT implementation straightforward, but implementing from scratch requires a lot of work. Use this if you're using established libraries; more complex if building from scratch.

Service accounts: Useful for automated systems and CI/CD. Too complex for initial evaluation.

Start simple, provide clear upgrade paths to more secure options as developers move toward production.

Samples and quickstarts

Sample applications and quickstarts serve different purposes, and understanding the difference helps you create better onboarding materials.

Quickstarts versus sample apps

Quickstarts are minimal examples designed to prove your product works in under five minutes. They're optimized for speed, not completeness. A quickstart might be 20 lines of code that makes a single API call and prints the result.

Sample applications are more complete examples that demonstrate real-world usage patterns. They show how to structure code, handle errors, and combine multiple features. Sample apps might be hundreds of lines showing a realistic integration.

Both have value, but they serve different stages of the developer journey. Quickstarts are for the five-minute window. Sample apps are for developers who've decided to build something real.

Creating effective quickstarts

The 5-minute quickstart formula:

1. One clear objective (for example, "Send your first SMS")
2. Minimal setup (one API key, no complex configuration)
3. Working code you can copy-paste and run
4. Immediate visible results
5. Clear explanation of what just happened
6. Logical next step

Anti-patterns to avoid:

Quickstarts that aren't quick. If it takes 20 minutes, it's not a quickstart.

Complex prerequisites. Requiring Docker, Kubernetes, or five environment variables defeats the purpose.

Examples that don't actually work. Test your quickstarts regularly. Broken examples destroy trust immediately.

Generic "hello world" that shows no real value. Balance simplicity with demonstrating actual capabilities.

Sample application best practices

Sample apps should showcase best practices and realistic patterns. Remember, developers will copy what you show them, so make it worth copying.

Show production-ready patterns from the start. Include error handling, retries, logging, and monitoring in your sample code. Yes, this makes examples longer and more complex, but it also teaches developers the right way to build from day one. When developers copy-paste your sample into their production code (and they will), you want them copying something that won't break at scale.

Demonstrate good architecture through clear code structure. Developers learn from your examples whether you intend them to or not. If your sample app is a messy pile of spaghetti code, that's what developers will build. If it's well-organized with clear separation of concerns, you're teaching good habits by example.

Configuration management matters more than you might think. Show developers how to handle secrets properly, manage environment variables, and configure for different environments. This is where many production issues originate, so teaching it early prevents pain later.

Include tests in your sample applications. Sample apps without tests send a clear message: testing isn't important. That's rarely the message you want to send. Even basic tests demonstrate that quality matters and show developers how to test integrations with your API.

Finally, write a README that explains your decisions. Don't just show the code, explain why you structured it this way and what trade-offs you made. Help developers understand the thinking behind the implementation. This context transforms a sample app from "code that works" into "code that teaches."

Real onboarding teardowns

Learning from others' successes provides valuable insights into what makes onboarding work. Let's examine how three different companies approach onboarding, each excelling in different ways.

Slack: Progressive disclosure done right

Slack's developer platform demonstrates how to guide developers through complexity without overwhelming them. Their quick-start walks through building a simple bot in stages, with each step building naturally on the previous one. They provide both high-level conceptual explanations and specific code examples, making it accessible to developers with varying experience levels.

What makes Slack's approach particularly effective is that it doesn't try to teach everything at once. You start with the simplest possible integration (incoming webhooks), then the platform shows you paths to more sophisticated apps as you're ready. This progressive complexity respects where developers are in their journey and meets them there.

Notion: Use case focusing at its best

Notion's API takes a different but equally effective approach. Instead of trying to cover every possible integration scenario, they provide specific, realistic examples like "sync your CRM contacts" or "create a simple dashboard." Each example includes complete code and clear explanations of the business value you're unlocking.

This use case-driven approach helps developers immediately connect the API to their actual needs. You're not learning abstract concepts, you're solving real problems that mirror what you actually want to build. The focus makes the learning curve feel manageable and relevant.

Twilio: The power of instant gratification

Twilio shows what happens when you prioritize immediate success above all else. Developers can send their first SMS within minutes of signing up. Even better, if you're not ready to code yet, you can use their web interface to experience that first win. This builds confidence before diving into API integration.

The instant gratification approach works because it proves the platform delivers value before asking for significant investment. Once developers see it work with their own eyes, they're much more motivated to do the harder work of integrating it properly into their applications.

Common patterns among successful onboarding

Across these three different approaches, several shared principles emerge. All three platforms demonstrate immediate value before requiring significant setup. They provide multiple entry points for different developer preferences and skill levels. Their error messages are clear and help developers self-correct rather than requiring support tickets. And they offer contextual help when and where developers need it, not buried in distant documentation pages.

The lesson here isn't to copy any one approach, but to understand that excellent onboarding comes in different forms. What works for Slack's complex bot platform differs from what works for Twilio's straightforward messaging API. The key is understanding your developers and your product, then designing an onboarding experience that fits both.

Metrics: Drop-off points and friction indicators

You can't improve what you don't measure. Onboarding metrics reveal where developers struggle and where you should invest effort.

Key onboarding metrics

Time to first API call. How long from landing on your docs to making their first successful request? Target: under 5 minutes for most APIs.

Quickstart completion rate. What percentage of developers who start your quickstart guide finish it? Target: above 60%.

First call success rate. What percentage of first API calls succeed versus error? Target: above 80%.

Setup abandonment points. Where do developers drop off during setup? Registration? API key creation? First code example?

Time to second call. Developers who make a second call within 24 hours are far more likely to activate. Track this carefully.

Error frequency in first session. High error rates during first sessions indicate documentation gaps or product issues.

Identifying friction points

Use multiple data sources to identify onboarding friction:

Analytics: Track page views, time on page, and drop-off points in your documentation.

Session recordings: Tools like FullStory or Hotjar show exactly where developers get stuck.

Support tickets: What questions come up most in first 24 hours? Each question represents a documentation gap.

User interviews: Talk to developers who recently onboarded. What was confusing? What almost made them quit?

Funnel analysis: Where do developers drop out between landing and activation? Each drop-off point is an opportunity for improvement.

Using metrics to drive improvement

Onboarding metrics only matter if they drive action:

1. **Identify the biggest drop-off point** in your funnel
2. **Form a hypothesis** about why developers are dropping off
3. **Make a specific change** to address that hypothesis
4. **Measure the impact** over the next week or two
5. **Iterate** based on results

Don't try to fix everything at once. Pick the highest-impact friction point and focus there until metrics improve.

Key takeaways

The five-minute window is real. Developers decide whether to invest in your product based on their first few minutes of experience. Make those minutes count.

Remove friction ruthlessly. Every unnecessary step, confusing instruction, or broken example costs you users. Optimize for the fastest path to value.

Start simple, layer complexity. Getting started should be trivially easy. Save the advanced features and configuration options for after developers have experienced initial success.

Test your own onboarding regularly. What's obvious to you is often confusing to newcomers. Fresh eyes catch problems you've stopped noticing.

Measure and iterate continuously. Track drop-off points, talk to users, and fix the biggest problems first. Onboarding is never "done."

Auth is often the biggest friction. Make authentication as simple as possible for getting started while providing clear paths to production-ready security.

In **Chapter 5**, we'll move beyond onboarding to explore how to help developers achieve real activation with your product, turning quick wins into meaningful production usage.

FIVE

Developer Activation: Success Beyond Hello World

HELP DEVELOPERS GO FROM EVALUATION TO PRODUCTION.

Getting developers through onboarding is a victory, but it's not the finish line. A developer who completes your Hello World tutorial but never uses your product in production has generated zero business value. Activation, the moment when a developer solves a real problem with your product using real data, is where evaluation transforms into genuine adoption.

This chapter explores how to bridge the gap between "it works in a tutorial" and "I'm using this in production." We'll cover use-case-driven documentation, SDKs and templates, production deployment patterns, and the scalable programs that help developers succeed beyond the basics.

What is activation?

Activation is the first moment a developer truly experiences the value of your product, not in a demo, but in their context. It's not when they sign up, run a test, or read the docs. It's when they solve a real problem, using your product, with their code, in their workflow.

At a high level:

Activation = first meaningful use

For a developer, this is a clear "aha!" moment, one that typically happens after onboarding, but before deep product engagement. It's the point where the product stops being interesting and starts being useful

> “At the end of your quickstart, give developers four or five clear next steps based on what successful users typically do next. Think about your ICP , what is that person likely to do when they complete onboarding? Bring that front and center, and let them self-guide in their own time."
>
> Jim Bennett (Principal Developer Experience Engineer, Arize AI)

Why activation matters

Activation is one of the most critical leverage points in the developer journey. A great onboarding flow might generate excitement, but it's meaningless if it doesn't lead to activation. DevRel programs that stop at awareness or tutorials often miss the business impact that comes from getting developers to production.

When developers don't activate, you get:

- Silent churn: developers leave before saying anything
- Inflated funnel metrics that never convert
- Wasted effort on content or SDKs that don't drive adoption

- Inaccurate feedback loops that slow product improvement

When developers do activate, you unlock:

- Increased trial-to-paid conversion
- Higher NPS and referral loops
- More meaningful product feedback
- Stronger usage data to guide your roadmap

Activation versus integration

It's important to distinguish between integration and activation. Integration may refer to dropping a code snippet or wiring up an SDK. Activation means the code is solving a real problem.

For example, a developer installs the Twilio SDK and sends a test SMS to themselves (integration). But they activate when they send password reset codes to their actual users in production.

Use-case-driven docs

Generic documentation explains what your API does. Use-case-driven documentation shows developers how to solve their specific problems. This shift from feature-focused to problem-focused documentation dramatically improves activation rates.

Understanding developer jobs to be done

Different developers have different jobs to be done, and a one-size-fits-all approach to documentation leaves everyone partially satisfied and no one fully served.

Think about how developers actually search for solutions. They don't think "I need to use the SMS API." They think "I need to verify users' phone numbers during signup." When you organize documentation around what developers are trying to accomplish rather than your product's features, you meet them where they are.

Consider the difference between these two approaches:

Feature-focused (weak): "SMS API Reference," "Voice API Reference," "Video API Reference"

Use-case-focused (strong): "Send verification codes," "Build customer support hotlines," "Add video calls to your app"

The second approach helps developers find solutions faster and shows them exactly how your product solves their problems. It's the difference between a parts catalog and a solution guide.

Creating use-case documentation

Effective use-case guides don't just document features, they solve problems. Start with the developer's pain point and walk them all the way to a working solution.

Begin with a clear problem statement that resonates with the developer's actual experience. "You need to verify users' phone numbers during signup" is much more concrete than "Learn about phone number verification." The developer should immediately recognize their own problem in your opening sentence.

Show the full implementation, not just the API calls. Include frontend code, backend logic, database interactions, everything a developer needs to actually ship this feature. Half-complete examples force developers to fill in the gaps, which introduces friction and increases the chance they'll implement it incorrectly.

Don't stop at the happy path. Production considerations matter. Cover error handling, rate limiting, retry logic, and scaling concerns. Developers who follow your tutorial need to build something that works in production, not just in a demo environment. When your documentation accounts for real-world complexity, you're setting developers up for success.

Show common variations of the solution. Different developers use different frameworks, languages, and architectures. When you demonstrate how to adapt your solution for Next.js versus Django versus Spring Boot, you're acknowledging that developers aren't all working in identical environments.

Include a troubleshooting section. Address the most common issues developers encounter when implementing this use case. This single addition can dramatically reduce support tickets and increase completion rates.

Organizing use-case docs

Organization matters as much as content. Developers need to find the right guide quickly, and your navigation should reflect how they think about problems.

Primary navigation should organize by developer intent: Getting Started, Common Use Cases, Advanced Patterns, and Reference. This structure mirrors the developer journey from "I'm just trying this out" to "I'm building something specific" to "I need to understand how this works under the hood."

Create a searchable use-case library where developers can filter by industry, language, framework, or feature combination. A developer building a React e-commerce app should be able to quickly find examples that match their exact context.

Cross-link between feature docs and use cases. Developers should easily move between "how it works" and "how to use it." Someone reading your SMS API reference might suddenly realize they need to see a complete verification code example. Make that jump effortless.

SDKs and code templates

SDKs and code templates reduce friction by giving developers battle-tested implementations instead of starting from scratch. But poorly designed SDKs can actually increase activation friction.

SDK design principles

The best SDKs feel native to the language they're written in. Python developers expect Pythonic code with clear, descriptive method names and proper use of Python idioms. JavaScript developers expect promises or async/await, not callback hell. Don't impose your API's patterns on the language's conventions. When your SDK fights against the language's natural style, every line of code becomes a small friction point.

Make the common case easy and the complex case possible. Developers should get value with minimal configuration. A good SDK lets someone make their first successful API call in three lines of code, then gracefully reveals more sophisticated options as they need them. Sensible defaults are your friend here, choose the settings that work for 80% of use cases and let developers override them when necessary.

When something goes wrong, your error messages should explain what happened, why it might have happened, and how to fix it. "Invalid API key" is technically accurate but not helpful. "Invalid

API key. Check that you're using your production key (starts with 'pk_live_') not your test key. Find your keys at https://dashboard.example.com/keys" actually helps developers recover. Clear error messages are the difference between a developer fixing their own issue in 30 seconds versus opening a support ticket.

Build documentation directly into your code. Type hints, JSDoc comments, and inline examples help developers discover functionality through their IDE without constantly switching to browser documentation. When a developer types your SDK's object name and sees autocomplete with helpful descriptions, that's excellent developer experience in action.

Automate SDK updates whenever possible. If you can auto-generate SDKs from your API spec (using tools like OpenAPI generators), do it. This ensures your SDKs stay in sync with your API as it evolves. Nothing frustrates developers more than an SDK that's missing features from the API or, worse, documents features that no longer exist.

Multi-language SDK strategy

Not every developer uses the same language, and you can't build excellent SDKs for every language that exists. So how do you decide which languages to support?

Start with your ICP. Focus on the language(s) your ideal customer profile uses most. If you're targeting mobile developers, Swift and Kotlin matter more than Ruby. If you're serving data scientists, Python takes priority over PHP. Don't guess, look at your actual users and prospects to understand what they're building with.

Quality over quantity. Three excellent SDKs beat seven mediocre ones every time. Unmaintained SDKs damage trust more than missing SDKs. A stale SDK with outdated examples and missing features tells developers you don't care about their experience. It's better to officially support fewer languages well than to half-heartedly support many.

For languages outside your core focus, support community-maintained SDKs rather than creating official but neglected ones. Provide clear guidelines, offer to link to community SDKs from your docs, and celebrate community contributors. Just be transparent that these are community-maintained, not officially supported.

Document your REST API well. When you have excellent REST API documentation, developers in any language can integrate even without an SDK. This gives you flexibility, you can focus your SDK efforts on your most important languages while still serving the long tail of developers working in niche languages.

> "We live in an SDK-first world, not an API-first world anymore. That means SDKs for Rust and Elixir as well as Java and .NET , broad coverage from the get-go."
>
> Zeno Rocha (Co-founder & CEO, Resend)

Code templates and starter projects

Beyond SDKs, provide complete starter projects that developers can clone and customize. These reduce time-to-value even further by giving developers a running application they can build on.

Framework-specific starters save developers hours of setup. A Next.js starter, Create React App template, Django template, or Spring Boot example, each pre-configured with your SDK, eliminates the integration work. Developers can focus on building their features instead of figuring out how to wire everything together.

Use-case templates go even further by providing complete implementations of common use cases. An authentication system, notification service, or payment flow that's ready to customize gives developers a huge head start. They can see your product in a realistic context and adapt the implementation to their specific needs.

Make your examples deploy-ready. Include deployment configurations for popular platforms like Vercel, Netlify, Heroku, and AWS. When developers can go from cloning your template to having it running in production in under an hour, you've dramatically increased the chance they'll activate.

Logging, debugging, and real-world deployment patterns

Tutorials show the happy path. Production requires handling errors, monitoring health, and debugging problems. Developers who can't troubleshoot issues won't reach activation.

Logging and observability

Help developers understand what's happening in production:

Structured logging examples. Show how to log API calls, responses, and errors in a structured format that's easy to search and analyze.

Request ID tracking. Every API call should return a request ID that developers can use to trace issues through your system and theirs.

Webhook debugging. Webhooks are particularly tricky to debug. Provide tools to inspect webhook payloads and retry failed deliveries.

Status pages and incidents. When your API has issues, developers need to know quickly. Maintain a public status page and communicate proactively during incidents.

Error handling patterns

Comprehensive error documentation. Document every error code your API returns, what causes it, and how to handle it.

Retry logic guidance. Which errors should developers retry? What's the recommended backoff strategy? Provide code examples.

Circuit breaker patterns. Show developers how to implement circuit breakers to protect their systems when your API is having issues.

Graceful degradation. Help developers design systems that continue to function, even if degraded, when your API is unavailable.

Production deployment patterns

Environment management. Show how to manage different API keys, configurations, and behaviors across development, staging, and production.

Security best practices. How should developers store API keys? What should never be committed to source control? Provide security checklists.

Performance optimization. Caching strategies, batch request patterns, and techniques to minimize latency and costs.

Monitoring and alerting. What should developers monitor? What thresholds warrant alerts? Provide CloudWatch, Datadog, or Prometheus configurations.

Scalable programs: training, workshops, developer tours, events

Not every developer learns through documentation alone. Scalable educational programs help developers activate through guided learning experiences.

Developer training programs

Different developers learn in different ways, and your training programs should reflect that diversity.

Self-paced courses give developers the flexibility to learn on their own schedule. Video tutorials, interactive exercises, and quizzes work well for developers who prefer to explore at their own pace, pausing and rewinding when they need to absorb complex concepts. The key is making them genuinely interactive, not just recorded lectures.

Live workshops create accountability and connection. Regular webinars that walk developers through specific use cases with live Q&A help developers who learn better with real-time guidance. The ability to ask questions and get immediate answers often makes the difference between understanding a concept and giving up in frustration.

Certification programs provide structure and motivation. When you create a formal learning path that validates developer expertise, you give developers a goal beyond just "figure out the API." Certifications also help developers justify learning time to their employers and build credentials that advance their careers.

Office hours remove barriers to asking for help. Setting regular times when your team is available to answer questions and help developers work through activation challenges creates a safety net. Many developers get stuck on small issues they could solve in minutes with the right guidance but instead spend hours struggling alone.

Developer tours and roadshows

Bringing DevRel in-person to developer communities creates connections that virtual interactions can't match.

Sponsoring local developer meetups puts you in front of developers in cities where your target audience gathers. These events are intimate enough for real conversations and large enough to make the trip worthwhile. You're not there to pitch, you're there to teach something valuable and build relationships.

Conference workshops offer concentrated learning experiences. Full-day or half-day hands-on sessions at developer conferences let you guide developers through complex implementations they wouldn't tackle on their own. The dedicated time and focused environment help developers break through activation barriers.

Hackathons drive rapid experimentation. Running or sponsoring hackathons focused on building with your platform creates intensity and excitement that documentation can't match. Developers build real projects in compressed timeframes, and you get to see how they actually use your platform under pressure.

University programs build long-term relationships. Partnering with computer science programs introduces students to your platform early in their careers. These developers may not activate immediately, but you're building awareness and familiarity that pays off years later when they're making platform decisions at companies.

Developer events

Events remain powerful activation tools, but the format matters as much as the content.

Virtual events scale better than in-person alternatives. Online events reach global audiences without travel costs, making them accessible to developers everywhere. But they lose the personal connection and serendipitous conversations that happen in hallways and over coffee. Use virtual events when reach matters more than depth of connection.

Hybrid events balance reach and connection. Streaming live events while maintaining in-person components for local communities gives you the best of both worlds. Remote developers can participate without travel, while local developers get the benefits of face-to-face interaction.

Event goals should be specific. Is this for awareness? Activation? Community building? Different goals require different event structures. An awareness event needs broad appeal and low barriers to entry. An activation event needs hands-on workshops and dedicated time for developers to build. A community event needs space for developers to connect with each other, not just with your team. Trying to accomplish all three goals in one event usually means accomplishing none of them well.

DevRel's role in activation

DevRel is uniquely positioned to drive activation because they're closest to the developer experience:

Developer empathy loops. DevRel interacts with real users via support, Discord, GitHub, and demos. They can identify confusion before it becomes churn.

Content that converts. Product docs explain what to do. DevRel shows how and why it matters, with working examples and opinionated walkthroughs.

Friction detectors. DevRel teams typically run Hello World tests internally or dogfood the onboarding. They're the first to detect inconsistencies.

Internal advocacy. DevRel can champion improvements to SDK ergonomics, docs structure, and error clarity, often before metrics expose the issue.

Metrics DevRel should monitor

- Time to first real API call
- Activation rate by referrer (which channels bring high-quality leads)
- Tutorial completion rate
- Support ticket to activation ratio

If DevRel doesn't own these metrics, no one will.

Key takeaways

Activation proves value in production, not theory. The gap between Hello World and real usage is where most developers get stuck. Bridge it intentionally.

Use-case-driven docs outperform feature-focused docs. Organize by developer jobs to be done, not your product's architecture.

SDKs reduce friction when done well. Idiomatic, well-documented SDKs with sensible defaults help developers succeed faster.

Production concerns can't be ignored. Error handling, logging, debugging, and deployment patterns determine whether developers reach activation.

Scalable programs extend reach. Training, workshops, and events help developers who don't learn through docs alone.

DevRel owns the activation ladder. Clear ownership of activation metrics, content, and friction detection makes the difference between random acts of advocacy and strategic developer success.

In **Chapter 6**, we'll explore how to transform activated users into an engaged community that learns together, answers each other's questions, and grows the ecosystem.

SIX

Engagement: Turning Activated Users Into Community

FROM EARLY ADOPTERS TO LIFELONG ADVOCATES.

By now, you've shipped Hello World and moved real projects toward production. Engagement is how you turn activated users into a community that learns together, answers each other's questions, and grows the ecosystem without you in the room. This chapter explores how to cultivate engagement that keeps developers connected, happy, and actively contributing to your ecosystem while skillfully navigating the inevitable challenges that arise.

Product-first community building

Before diving into community tactics, it's crucial to understand a fundamental truth: community is downstream of product quality. No amount of community building can compensate for a poor developer experience, and conversely, truly great products will naturally attract communities regardless of your efforts.

Recognition often motivates continued participation more effectively than manufactured incentives.

The foundation of authentic engagement

The product-first approach creates the foundation for authentic community engagement. When developers gather because they genuinely value your platform, their interactions are more meaningful, their contributions are more substantial, and their advocacy is more credible.

This doesn't mean you should wait for perfect product-market fit before engaging with your community. Instead, it means being honest about where you are in your journey and focusing community efforts on understanding and serving real user needs rather than creating artificial engagement.

> "Often you think of community as being authentic and organic, and yet, at the same time, if you're thinking about tooling, staffing, what the intent of the community is, how you're going to drive engagement, that all has strategy behind it."
>
> Katie Miller (Dev Marketing Leader, former Google/Slack)

Support systems that scale

> "One of the things that we did really well at the beginning was make support a big priority. Anyone who values where the platform is really needs to think hard about making sure that you fund and support a developer support function. And then make sure that there is a tight integration with the rest of developer relations, because that is a super strong signal to what's happening."

Jim Ray (Director, Developer Advocacy, Slack, Bluesky)

Tiered support architecture

Effective community support requires a multi-layered approach that can handle everything from basic questions to complex technical challenges. The most successful communities implement a tiered system:

Community self-service. Start with comprehensive documentation, FAQs, and searchable knowledge bases. These resources should be easily discoverable and regularly updated based on common support patterns.

Peer-to-peer support. Foster an environment where experienced developers help newcomers. This can be facilitated through forums, Discord servers, or dedicated channels in your community platform. The key is making it easy for helpers to find questions they can answer and providing recognition for their contributions.

Expert office hours. Regular sessions where your team members are available for real-time questions create predictable touchpoints for deeper engagement. These can be scheduled weekly video calls, live streaming sessions, or dedicated chat hours.

Escalation pathways. For complex issues that require internal expertise, provide clear escalation paths so developers aren't left in limbo.

Building a culture of helpfulness

The tone you set in your community profoundly impacts how developers interact with each other. Thriving communities emphasize that no question is too basic, helpful community members are celebrated, and there's a welcoming environment for developers of all skill levels.

Consider implementing recognition systems that highlight community members who consistently provide valuable help. This could be as simple as monthly "community hero" spotlights or as structured as point-based systems that unlock special privileges.

> "Open source has allowed communities to start forming. Before open source, hardware development was very insular with company secrets and proprietary software."
>
> Jonathan Beri (Founder, Golioth; ex-Google IoT)

Champion and ambassador programs

Champion and ambassador programs formalize relationships with your most engaged developers, transforming them into external advocates and experts. These programs create a multiplier effect: champions drive awareness through their networks, elevate proficiency by teaching others, and provide authentic advocacy that carries far more weight than any marketing message. When structured well, these programs scale your DevRel efforts exponentially while deepening relationships with developers who genuinely love your platform.

Identifying natural leaders

Every community contains individuals who naturally gravitate toward helping others, sharing knowledge, and advocating for the platform. These developers are goldmines for building scalable community engagement.

Look for developers who:

- Consistently provide helpful answers in community forums
- Create and share tutorials or content about your platform
- Speak at meetups or conferences about your technology
- Contribute to open-source projects related to your ecosystem
- Demonstrate deep technical knowledge combined with teaching ability

Structured ambassador programs

Once you've identified potential champions, create formal structures to support and amplify their efforts:

Microsoft MVP-style programs. Provide recognition, exclusive access to product teams, advance notice of new features, and opportunities to influence product direction. The key is making ambassadors feel like true partners rather than just users.

Content creation support. Offer resources like technical reviews, promotional support, or financial compensation for high-quality content creation. This might include blog posts, video tutorials, or conference presentations.

Product feedback loops. Create dedicated channels where champions can provide direct feedback to product teams. This makes them feel valued while giving you insights from your most engaged users.

Community moderation. Empower trusted community members to help moderate discussions, welcome newcomers, and maintain community standards. This scales your team's impact while giving champions meaningful ways to contribute.

> "In the end you're trying to create champions. I think the biggest thing with a developer champion is when a developer starts to love you, they are some of the best-paid people at their company. So when they fight for your product, you win a lot of the time. Minting those champions is critical with developers."
>
> Cecilia Stallsmith (Head of Marketing, Lovable)

Beta programs and feedback loops

Beta programs are essential for gathering early feedback before features reach your entire user base. They help you find bugs and edge cases that are nearly impossible to spot without real-world usage, no matter how thorough your internal testing. Beyond quality assurance, beta programs serve as a strategic onboarding mechanism, getting key partners familiar with new features before they launch publicly. This early access transforms beta participants into informed advocates who can hit the ground running on launch day.

Early access as community building

Successful beta programs require structure and communication. Start with a kickoff session that sets clear expectations and goals. Then maintain momentum through regular check-ins, weekly async updates work well for most programs. Finally, close the loop publicly by sharing what changed based on beta feedback. This transparency shows participants their input mattered and encourages future engagement.

Structured beta onboarding. Don't just grant access. Create orientation sessions to help beta participants understand not just what to test, but why their feedback matters and how to provide helpful input.

Regular check-ins. Schedule consistent touchpoints throughout the beta period. These might be weekly calls, async updates, or structured surveys to keep participants engaged and ensure you're capturing valuable feedback.

Post-beta recognition. When features launch, publicly acknowledge beta participants' contributions. This recognition motivates future participation and demonstrates that community input has real impact.

Building feedback loops that work

Effective feedback collection requires systems that make it easy for developers to share insights while ensuring that input actually influences product decisions.

Multiple feedback channels. Different developers prefer different communication methods. Offer options including forums, surveys, direct emails, video calls, and in-person meetings for local community members.

Transparent communication. Share how feedback is being used, what changes are being made based on community input, and why certain suggestions might not be implemented. This transparency builds trust and encourages continued participation.

Product roadmap integration. Create formal processes for incorporating community feedback into product planning. This might include quarterly roadmap reviews with community input or regular feature prioritization sessions with champion groups.

Forums, Discord, and office hours

Choosing the right platforms

Different community platforms serve various purposes and attract different types of engagement:

Traditional forums. Excellent for structured, searchable discussions that provide long-term value. Topics remain discoverable and can be referenced months or years later.

Discord and Slack. Great for real-time interaction, quick questions, and building personal connections. These platforms excel at creating immediate engagement but require more active moderation.

Office hours. Whether conducted over video calls, live streams, or chat sessions, regular office hours create predictable opportunities for deeper engagement with your team.

Most successful communities use multiple platforms strategically rather than trying to force all interaction into a single channel.

Moderation and community standards

Effective moderation isn't about controlling conversations. It's about creating environments where productive discussion can flourish.

Clear community guidelines. Establish and communicate standards for behavior, discussion topics, and content sharing. Make these guidelines easily accessible and regularly referenced.

Proactive moderation. Don't wait for problems to escalate. Active community management includes welcoming new members, redirecting off-topic discussions, and addressing conflicts before they become toxic.

Empowering community moderation. Train trusted community members to help with moderation duties. This scales your efforts while giving active participants meaningful ways to contribute.

Meetups and self-sustaining communities

Meetups represent one of the most powerful yet misunderstood community engagement strategies. When done well, they create self-sustaining networks of developers who teach and support each other without requiring your constant presence.

Google Developer Groups (GDG) demonstrate the potential scale. With more than 250 independent groups of developers around the world, Google built a community that runs on local leadership and shared principles. Each GDG community meets regularly, usually monthly, running evening events with speakers discussing Google technologies. The meetup cadence becomes the heartbeat of the community, and community leaders measure their success by consistency as much as attendance.

The scalability model

The magic of meetup programs is their efficiency. You can run hundreds of meetups around the world with just one to three full-time community managers. This scalability comes from empowering local volunteer leaders to own their communities while you provide the framework and support.

Your role shifts from running events to enabling others to run them. You might sponsor pizza, provide technical content, or offer swag, but you're not flying to every city to present. Community managers scout for new local volunteer leaders, outline community principles that guide behavior and goals, create community assets like websites and training materials, and communicate with each local community to monitor health and provide support when needed.

> "It's all about building community. You need a community to fuel large-scale API adoption. A lot of APIs, like ours, are self-serve. If it's self serve, it needs to be super easy to grasp and use. The Facebook SDK got wide adoption because it was a feature that people needed, but the community helped to make it what it is today. You want to respect the power of community, they talk about benefits, they help each other. One of our groups, Facebook for Developers, has six million members and is really moderated by the community. It's a strong thing to have in this ecosystem. Value your community. While solid support and documentation is a cornerstone to any API adoption, the power of community should never be underestimated."
>
> Desiree Motamedi (Developer Marketing, Facebook)

When to build your own community versus joining existing ones

Not every API requires a separate community of its own. Before investing in building a community from scratch, consider whether you can offer your content to an existing community, especially if the community members would benefit from that content.

For example, the Unity team (game API) provides content for game hackathons with Android Developer Groups rather than building an entirely separate Unity community. This approach gives them access to relevant developers without the overhead of managing their own meetup network.

Build your own community when:

- Your platform is substantial enough to support regular, unique content
- You have sufficient users to sustain local groups in multiple cities
- Your technology warrants dedicated discussion separate from broader topics
- You can commit to supporting community leaders long-term

Join or support existing communities when:

- You're early stage with a smaller user base
- Your technology complements rather than defines a developer's focus
- Relevant communities already exist and welcome your participation
- Resource constraints limit your ability to support independent community leaders

Hackathons and ecosystem challenges

Beyond one-off events

Traditional hackathons generate excitement and awareness in concentrated bursts. Developers show up, build frantically for 24 or 48 hours, maybe win a prize, and then... often nothing. The energy dissipates when the event ends.

The most successful communities think bigger than one-off events. Instead of running a single annual hackathon, consider monthly or quarterly challenges that explore different aspects of your platform. This creates ongoing engagement while allowing participants to build skills progressively. Each challenge becomes a building block rather than an isolated experience.

Provide regular opportunities for developers to share their creations. Demo days, blog features, conference presentations, recognition motivates continued participation. Developers want their work seen and appreciated. When you create showcase moments, you're giving participants a reason to keep building and improving.

Facilitate longer-term collaborative projects where community members work together on substantial applications or tools. These projects create deeper connections than solo hackathon sprints ever could. Developers form relationships, learn from each other, and produce more meaningful contributions. The social bonds formed through collaboration often outlast the projects themselves.

Measuring challenge success

Don't fall into the trap of measuring success by participation counts alone. A hundred developers showing up means nothing if none of them continue engaging after the event ends.

Focus on engagement depth instead. Track how many participants actually complete challenges, continue building after events end, and engage with subsequent community activities. These behaviors indicate real impact rather than superficial interest.

Measure skill development too. Did participants demonstrate increased platform knowledge? Did they advance through your developer funnel after participating? If developers aren't learning and growing, your challenges aren't working.

Assess community connection. Challenge participants should become more active in forums, contribute to discussions, and potentially take on community leadership roles. The best hackathons and challenges don't just produce code, they produce community members who stick around and help others.

Key takeaways

Product quality comes first. Community is downstream of product quality. No amount of community building compensates for poor developer experience.

Support that scales has tiers. Self-service, peer support, office hours, and escalation paths create systems that handle volume while maintaining quality.

Champions multiply impact. Natural leaders in your community can scale support, content, and advocacy far beyond what your team can do alone.

Beta programs build relationships. Early access programs done well create invested advocates while providing valuable product feedback.

Platform choice matters. Forums for searchable knowledge, Discord for real-time help, office hours for deep engagement. Use the right tool for each purpose.

Moderation enables growth. Clear guidelines and proactive moderation create safe spaces where helpful, productive communities flourish.

Engagement isn't a social nice-to-have. It's how you scale developer success. In ☞ **Chapter 7**, we'll explore how to turn this trust into value exchange without breaking the social contract.

SEVEN

Monetization: Driving Value Without Selling Out

WHERE DEVREL MEETS REVENUE, WITHOUT BECOMING SALES.

DevRel sits at the intersection of growth and revenue, but it isn't sales. DevRel earns trust, removes friction, and proves value so commercial conversations happen naturally when developers are ready. In this chapter, we show how to turn healthy usage and community momentum into sustainable monetization without eroding trust.

The DevRel revenue relationship

DevRel has a complex relationship with monetization. Done wrong, it destroys trust and turns advocates into salespeople. Done right, it creates sustainable growth engines that benefit developers and the business.

DevRel isn't a sales organization. Many companies get this critical distinction wrong. DevRel should never be measured on sales metrics, carry quotas, or be expected to close deals. The moment DevRel becomes a sales function, it loses its most valuable asset: developer trust.

> "You're not tying it to revenue or to leads. You're tying it to the growth of the developers. If that's a core thing for the business model, it's easy to gain investment into those spaces."
>
> Simon Maple (Head of Developer Relations, Tessl)

Instead, DevRel drives revenue indirectly through:

- **Reducing acquisition costs** by building organic awareness and trust
- **Increasing conversion rates** through better onboarding and education
- **Expanding usage** by helping developers discover new use cases
- **Improving retention** through community engagement and support
- **Creating network effects** where successful developers attract others

DevRel's role isn't to sell but to remove friction from the developer journey and create conditions where natural monetization can occur. Sales should be done by people who are trained, equipped, and measured for that purpose.

The adoption-monetization tension

DevRel exists in a fundamental tension: you need developers to adopt your platform freely while also generating revenue to sustain the business. Get this balance wrong, and you either starve the company or kill adoption. Get it right, and you create a sustainable ecosystem where value flows in both directions.

The paywall problem

Developers need to experience value before they're willing to pay for it. Put up a paywall too early, and you kill onboarding before it starts. Developers won't commit time and effort to learning a platform when they can't even validate whether it solves their problem.

This creates a tricky design challenge. You need developers to get far enough into your platform to see real value, but you also need to convert them to paying customers at some point. The most successful platforms let developers build and test real use cases before requiring payment. They prove value first, then ask for money.

Stripe gets this right. You can integrate their entire payment system, test with their sandbox, and build a complete implementation before processing a single real transaction. By the time you're ready to go live, you've already invested enough that switching would be painful, and more importantly, you've seen the value firsthand.

Pricing complexity kills conversion

If developers can't understand your pricing in under two minutes, they'll walk away. Complex pricing models with multiple tiers, confusing usage calculations, and hidden costs create friction that kills conversion.

Developers are already evaluating whether your technical solution is worth the integration effort. Adding pricing complexity on top of technical complexity is asking them to solve two hard problems simultaneously. Most won't bother.

Keep pricing transparent and predictable. Show clear examples of what typical usage costs. Provide calculators that let developers estimate their bills before committing. Eliminate surprises. When developers can confidently predict costs, they're more likely to commit.

The sales perception problem

The moment developers perceive DevRel as sales, they stop engaging. This isn't about developers being difficult, it's about respecting the relationship you've built through education and support.

Developers come to DevRel for technical help, honest advice, and authentic community. When that relationship shifts to sales pressure, trust evaporates. Developers who were happily asking technical questions suddenly disappear. They'll self-serve through documentation rather than risk a sales pitch.

This is why DevRel should never carry quotas or be measured on closed deals. The value DevRel provides is creating the conditions where commercial conversations happen naturally when developers are ready. Pushing sales conversations before developers are ready destroys that value.

Self-service over sales conversations

Developers overwhelmingly prefer to evaluate, integrate, and even purchase without talking to a salesperson. This isn't universal, enterprise deals often require sales engagement, but for most developers, the ideal path is entirely self-service.

Consider Slack's experience: their marketing landing page for developers received 3% of the traffic that their API specification documentation received. Developers don't want marketing content. They want technical details that help them evaluate whether the platform solves their problem.

Design your monetization around this preference. Make it easy to start a free trial without talking to anyone. Provide clear upgrade paths that developers can execute themselves. Create pricing pages that answer technical questions, not just business questions. Let developers buy when they're ready, not when your sales team is ready to sell.

Content that sells by not selling

Sales-oriented content gets ignored by developers. Feature-benefit marketing copy, comparison charts filled with checkmarks, and polished testimonials from executives, all of this bounces off developer audiences.

What works instead is content that solves problems. Technical tutorials that happen to use your paid features. Architecture guides that demonstrate scaling patterns available in higher tiers. Case studies that show real implementation details, not just results.

The best developer-focused content earns attention by being genuinely useful, and it drives revenue by naturally demonstrating the value of paid features. Developers upgrade because they've already experienced the value, not because they've been convinced by marketing copy.

The free-to-paid transition trap

Moving from free or open source to paid models requires extreme care. Developers who built on your free platform feel betrayed when features suddenly move behind paywalls. This isn't about developers being entitled, it's about respecting the implicit contract you established.

Redis, Docker, and many open source projects have faced backlash when changing licensing or pricing models. The pattern is predictable: existing users feel like they've been hit with a bait-and-switch. Trust erodes quickly, and vocal advocates can turn into equally vocal critics.

If you need to transition from free to paid, do it thoughtfully:

- Give existing users generous grandfather periods
- Be transparent about why the change is necessary
- Ensure the free tier remains genuinely useful
- Add value to paid tiers rather than removing value from free tiers
- Communicate changes well in advance

The developers you've attracted with free offerings are your most important users. Handle the transition poorly, and you lose not just their usage but their advocacy and trust.

Understanding developer monetization models

Different business models require different DevRel approaches to monetization.

Freemium model

In freemium models, DevRel focuses on driving developers through the free tier to paid usage. This requires:

Generous free tiers that allow real experimentation and prototyping **Clear value demonstrations** showing when and why developers should upgrade

Usage education helps developers understand optimization strategies **Success amplification** showcasing developers who've grown with the platform

The goal is to make the upgrade feel natural rather than forced. When developers succeed with free tiers, they organically hit limits that justify paid plans.

Usage-based pricing

For products with usage-based pricing, DevRel's role is to maximize healthy usage growth:

Optimization guidance helps developers use APIs efficiently **Use case expansion** shows new ways to leverage the platform **Integration depth** encourages more comprehensive implementations **Performance education** teaches best practices that drive usage

Success here means developers use more of the API because they're getting more value, not because they're wasteful.

Enterprise pricing

For many platforms, enterprise deals represent what they ultimately aspire to sell. While developers may start with freemium tiers or usage-based models, the real revenue driver often comes from negotiated enterprise agreements.

Enterprise pricing typically involves custom negotiations rather than self-service sign-ups. These deals can be highly lucrative, a million-dollar contract for unlimited users accessing the platform for internal enterprise use isn't uncommon. The pricing structure moves away from per-user or per-API-call models toward flat enterprise licenses that provide predictability for both parties.

DevRel's role in enterprise sales is indirect but crucial. You're not closing the deals, but you're creating the conditions that make them possible:

Bottom-up adoption where individual developers prove value within their organizations **Champions creation** by identifying and supporting influential developers who become internal advocates **Organizational spread** as successful implementations expand to other teams **Executive awareness** through case studies and success stories that reach decision-makers

The enterprise sales motion often begins with a single developer trying out your platform on a small project. If that developer succeeds and the integration proves valuable, usage spreads. Eventually, someone in procurement or leadership notices significant spend or usage and initiates a conversation about an enterprise agreement.

Your job is to make that developer's initial experience so successful that they become an internal champion fighting for your platform at the organizational level. When the enterprise sales team finally gets involved, the technical decision has often already been made by the developers who are already depending on your platform.

Compliance considerations for enterprise: Enterprise contracts often require compliance certifications (SOC 2, HIPAA, GDPR, etc.) that startups may not have initially. While you shouldn't let compliance block your early product development, you need a strategy for when to invest.

> "You can try and wing compliance, and you'll probably get along for a while. But if you want large enterprise contracts, you will eventually need to fall into a certain compliance regime. My recommendation: focus on product, but do not overlook compliance completely. At least be aware, understand the requirements, do the design, and then make a call on how much to invest and when."
>
> Yochay Kiriaty (Director of Product Management, Google Kubernetes Engine)

Subscription models

With subscription APIs, DevRel focuses on providing ongoing value:

Feature adoption ensures that developers use all relevant capabilities **Success metrics** help developers measure ROI from the platform **Community engagement** creates stickiness through relationships **Renewal readiness** maintains active, successful developer relationships

The emphasis is on delivering continuous value rather than achieving one-time conversions.

Open source plus commercial

For open-source companies, DevRel bridges the gap between free and paid:

Community cultivation builds strong open-source adoption **Commercial awareness** educates about enterprise features **Migration paths** smooth transitions from open source to commercial **Value differentiation** explains commercial benefits clearly

This model requires careful balance between community interests and business needs.

Open Source and Open-Core Business Models

Open source fundamentally changes the DevRel equation. When your code is public, your community can fork it, your competitors can use it, and your business model must look beyond software licensing. Yet some of the most successful developer platforms, from Linux to Android to Kong, are built on open source foundations.

Understanding when and how to build on open source isn't just a licensing decision. It's a strategic choice that shapes your entire DevRel approach, community dynamics, and path to sustainability.

The open source spectrum

Open source isn't a single model. It's a spectrum of approaches, each with different implications for how you build community and drive revenue.

Pure open source (Linux, Kubernetes) releases all code under permissive licenses with no commercial product. The Linux Foundation maintains Linux through a governance model where multiple companies contribute because they all benefit from a shared infrastructure. DevRel in this model focuses entirely on contributor growth, technical quality, and ecosystem expansion. There's no monetization stage in the traditional sense, sustainability comes from corporate sponsorship and foundation support.

Linus Torvalds doesn't sell Linux. He maintains quality, coordinates contributors, and protects the project's technical direction. DevRel for pure open source means building contributor pipelines, maintaining governance structures, and ensuring the project serves its community's needs rather than any single company's agenda.

Open platforms (Android) release core code as open source while maintaining strategic control and monetizing through ecosystem services. Google open-sourced Android but maintains its direction, ships Google Play Services as proprietary, and monetizes through app store revenue and services integration.

Android's DevRel serves two audiences simultaneously: device manufacturers who build on Android (hardware ecosystem) and app developers who build for Android (software ecosystem). The platform is free, but Google's business model relies on maintaining enough control to drive users toward Google services while keeping the platform open enough that manufacturers adopt it globally.

This creates unique DevRel challenges. You're building community around code you control but don't exclusively own. Samsung can fork Android (and has, with Tizen), but they choose not to because the ecosystem value of staying compatible with mainline Android exceeds the value of going independent.

Open-core (Kong, GitLab, Elastic) releases a feature-complete core product as open source while selling proprietary enterprise features, hosting, or support. Kong's API Gateway core is Apache 2.0 licensed and powers thousands of companies. Kong Inc. monetizes through Kong Enterprise (with features like

RBAC, advanced plugins, and dedicated support) and Kong Konnect (their hosted/managed service).

This model creates inherent tension. Your open-source community wants features that you're trying to sell. GitLab navigated this by publishing their product tiers openly and being transparent about which features stay open source versus which move to paid tiers. The key is ensuring your open-source tier remains genuinely useful, not crippled to drive upgrades.

DevRel in open-core models must balance community cultivation (driving open-source adoption) with commercial awareness (educating about paid features without alienating the community). You're simultaneously building community trust and creating upgrade paths.

Open protocols (Bluesky AT Protocol) publish specifications that anyone can implement, creating decentralized ecosystems where multiple companies and projects compete and interoperate. Bluesky developed the AT Protocol (Authenticated Transfer Protocol) as an open standard for decentralized social networking. Anyone can run their own AT Protocol server, build their own client, or create their own algorithmic feeds.

This model separates protocol governance from commercial implementation. Bluesky PBC (the company) maintains the protocol and builds the flagship Bluesky app, but the protocol's success depends on multiple independent implementations thriving. DevRel here focuses on protocol adoption, reference implementation quality, and helping diverse teams build interoperable services.

The monetization challenge is unique: you're not selling the protocol or even necessarily a specific implementation. You might monetize through hosting, premium features in your implementation, or by building valuable services on top of the open protocol.

When to choose open source

Open source isn't right for every developer platform, but it creates powerful advantages when conditions align:

Network effects and ecosystem lock-in matter more than code secrecy. If your competitive advantage comes from the ecosystem built around your platform rather than secret algorithms, open source accelerates adoption. Android won mobile not because Google's code was better, but because opening it created an ecosystem of device manufacturers, app developers, and contributors that iOS couldn't match on reach.

You need rapid adoption in competitive markets. Closed-source developer tools face a chicken-and-egg problem: developers won't commit time to learning your platform until they see adoption, but adoption requires developers to invest time. Open source removes adoption friction by eliminating licensing costs, enabling evaluation without sales conversations, and allowing developers to inspect and modify code.

Kong competed against proprietary API gateways by being open source. Companies could deploy Kong immediately, customize it for their needs, and scale without worrying about licensing costs. By the time they needed enterprise features, they'd already standardized on Kong.

Your business model can work without software licensing revenue. Open source forces you to find revenue models beyond selling software licenses. This might mean selling support and services (Red Hat), hosting and management (Elastic Cloud), enterprise features (GitLab), or ecosystem services

(Google with Android). If your unit economics depend on per-seat software licensing, open source probably doesn't work.

You want to build a contributor ecosystem. Open source enables external contributors to improve your product, fix bugs, and add features you'd never prioritize. Linux has thousands of contributors across hundreds of companies. No single company could match this development velocity.

DevRel strategies by open source model

Different open source models require fundamentally different DevRel approaches.

For pure open source projects:

Focus entirely on contributor growth and project health. Your metrics are commits, contributors, and project activity, not revenue. Create clear contribution guidelines that reduce friction for first-time contributors. Linux uses detailed documentation and maintainer trees that help new contributors understand where and how to contribute.

Build governance structures that balance influence fairly. The Linux Foundation prevents any single company from dominating the project's direction. Kubernetes uses a similar model with SIGs (Special Interest Groups) that distribute technical decision-making.

Celebrate contributors publicly and create paths from occasional contributor to maintainer to project leadership. Recognition matters more than compensation in volunteer-driven projects.

For open platforms:

Serve two distinct audiences without conflating them. Android DevRel teams run separate programs for device manufacturers (Android Partner programs) and app developers (Google Play developer programs). The needs are completely different.

Maintain platform quality while encouraging ecosystem diversity. Google's Android Compatibility Test Suite ensures devices meet baseline standards while allowing manufacturers to customize and differentiate.

Balance platform control with community needs. When Google tried to push Google Play Services too aggressively, the Android community pushed back. Effective platform DevRel listens to ecosystem feedback even when it conflicts with the platform owner's short-term interests.

For open-core businesses:

Maintain crystal-clear boundaries between open source and commercial features. GitLab publishes what's open source versus paid in their public repository. Kong documents which features are community versus enterprise in their docs. Ambiguity breeds resentment.

Build the open-source tier as a genuinely useful product, not a crippled trial. Your open-source users are your community, your contributors, and your advocates. If they feel the open-source version is deliberately hobbled to force upgrades, you lose their trust and advocacy.

Create upgrade paths that feel natural rather than forced. Developers should upgrade because they've outgrown open-source capabilities (need enterprise SSO, advanced RBAC, dedicated support), not because you've artificially limited the open-source tier.

Contribute meaningfully to your own open-source project. Kong's engineering team ships features to open-source Kong, not just Kong Enterprise. This demonstrates commitment to the community rather than just extracting value from it.

For open protocols:

Focus on reference implementation quality and interoperability. The protocol's success depends on multiple teams building compatible implementations. Bluesky maintains atproto libraries and reference servers that make building AT Protocol-compatible services easier.

Build educational resources that help developers understand the protocol's design philosophy, not just its API surface. Protocol adoption requires deeper understanding than API integration.

Foster ecosystem diversity rather than pushing a single implementation. Your success comes from protocol adoption across many implementations, not just users of your specific product.

The governance question

Open source projects need governance structures that balance community input with sustainable decision-making. Poor governance kills projects through either tyranny (one company dominates) or paralysis (no one can make decisions).

Benevolent dictator model (Linux): Linus Torvalds has final say on what enters the Linux kernel. This works because Linus has earned community trust over decades and exercises authority judiciously. Most projects shouldn't attempt this model, it only works with rare individuals who combine technical excellence, earned authority, and community respect.

Foundation model (Linux Foundation, Cloud Native Computing Foundation): Neutral foundations host projects, provide governance frameworks, and prevent single-company dominance. Kubernetes moved to the CNCF to ensure Google wouldn't be perceived as controlling its direction. Foundations work when multiple companies have strategic interest in the project's success.

Company-led open source (Android, Kong): A single company maintains the project but accepts contributions and considers community input. This is fastest for decision-making but requires careful attention to community trust. Google maintains Android's direction but must balance that control with manufacturer and developer needs.

Common open source pitfalls

Even well-intentioned open source initiatives fail when they ignore these patterns:

The "open source as marketing" trap: Releasing code as open source purely to generate buzz, then abandoning it when it doesn't drive immediate adoption. An unmaintained open-source project damages your reputation more than never releasing it.

The license switcheroo: Launching as open source, building community adoption, then changing to restrictive licenses when you want to monetize. Redis, MongoDB, and Elastic all faced community backlash after license changes. If you're planning eventual license restrictions, be transparent from the start.

The hollow open-source tier: Making the open-source version so limited that it's unusable in production, forcing upgrades to access basic functionality. This breeds resentment rather than commercial conversion.

Ignoring contributor needs: Treating external contributors as free labor rather than community partners. Rejected pull requests without explanation, ignored issues, and closed decision-making kill contribution pipelines.

Confusing open source with free support: Expecting unpaid maintainers to provide enterprise-grade support to commercial users. Open source means the code is open; it doesn't mean unlimited free support.

Making open source sustainable

The hardest challenge in open source isn't building community, it's sustaining it long-term. Projects fail not from lack of interest but from burnout, funding gaps, or inability to monetize.

For pure open source: Foundation funding, corporate sponsorship, and paid maintainer positions. Linux Foundation member companies fund kernel development. CNCF member fees support Kubernetes infrastructure.

For open platforms: Monetize ecosystem services, not the platform itself. Google doesn't charge for Android; they monetize through Google Play, ads, and services integration.

For open-core: Build genuinely valuable commercial features that serve real enterprise needs. Kong Enterprise adds SSO, advanced analytics, and dedicated support, features that enterprises need and hobbyists don't.

For open protocols: Monetize implementations, hosting, or premium services built on the protocol. Bluesky will likely monetize through hosting services, moderation tools, or premium features in their app while keeping the protocol open.

DevRel's role in driving usage

DevRel impacts usage through multiple channels, but always indirectly. The focus is on promoting healthy usage patterns that benefit developers instead of pushing for maximum consumption.

Healthy usage versus sales-driven usage is a crucial distinction. DevRel should never encourage wasteful or inefficient API usage just to drive revenue. Instead, focus on:

- **Sustainable implementations** to solve real developer problems
- **Efficient usage patterns** to optimize for developer success
- **Value-driven adoption** where increased usage reflects increased value
- **Long-term developer success** rather than short-term consumption spikes

This approach fosters trust and promotes sustainable growth, whereas sales-driven tactics can erode community relationships.

> "We do a lot of activities without fully justifying them because we know it's the right thing to do. We want to do things the right way."
>
> Simon Maple (Head of Developer Relations, Tessl)

The DevRel-sales collaboration model

While DevRel isn't a sales organization, it must work closely with sales teams to drive business results. The key is maintaining clear boundaries and complementary roles.

DevRel responsibilities

- Community building and developer relationship management
- Education and enablement through content and events
- Product feedback collection and advocacy
- Usage optimization guidance and best practices
- Trust building through authentic developer advocacy

Sales responsibilities

- Lead qualification and opportunity management
- Commercial negotiations and contract discussions
- Revenue targets and quota achievement
- Customer relationships focused on business outcomes
- Deal closure and commercial success

Collaboration points

The most effective model involves clear handoff points:

- **Qualified leads** from DevRel to sales when developers express commercial interest
- **Technical expertise** from DevRel to support sales conversations
- **Success stories** from sales back to DevRel for community amplification
- **Product feedback** from sales to DevRel for ecosystem improvement

DevRel opens the door and proves fit. Sales walks through it and closes. Mixing roles creates either bad DevRel or bad sales.

> "Eventually I had to tell them, you know, I'm not on the sales team. I can't go on every customer call."
>
> Jim Ray (Director, Developer Advocacy, Slack, Bluesky)

Balancing community and commerce

The most challenging aspect of DevRel monetization is maintaining authentic community relationships while driving business results. You're walking a tightrope, lean too far toward commerce and you lose community trust; lean too far toward community and you can't sustain the business.

Trust preservation

Community trust is DevRel's most valuable asset, and it's far easier to lose than to build. Once developers stop trusting you, almost nothing you do will matter because they simply won't listen.

Transparency about your business goals and monetization approach goes a long way. Developers understand that companies need to make money. What they don't tolerate is pretending you're purely there to help while secretly optimizing for conversions. Be honest about how you make money and why certain features are paid.

Practice authentic advocacy by genuinely caring about developer success, not just about getting them to the next tier. When you recommend solutions, recommend what's actually best for the developer, even if that sometimes means suggesting a competitor or acknowledging your platform isn't the right fit. This honesty builds more trust than any amount of feature promotion.

Your actions must align with your stated values. If you say "developers first" but constantly push sales agendas, developers notice the inconsistency immediately. Consistent messaging means walking the talk, especially when it's inconvenient for your quarterly targets.

Balance community interests with business needs rather than treating them as opposing forces. Often, what's genuinely good for developers is also good for the business, just on a longer timeline than sales would prefer. Prioritize sustainable growth over quarterly spikes.

Ethical monetization

Sustainable monetization benefits developers and the business in equal measure. When either party feels exploited, the relationship breaks down.

Ensure developers get fair value for their investment. Your pricing should reflect the value you provide, not just what you can extract from developers who've become dependent on your platform. Developers who feel they're paying a fair price become vocal advocates. Developers who feel gouged become vocal critics.

Avoid exploiting developer dependence. Yes, switching costs create pricing power, but using that power to dramatically raise prices or restrict previously free features destroys goodwill. The short-term revenue gain rarely compensates for the long-term reputation damage.

Be honest about costs and limitations upfront. Hidden fees, surprise rate limits, and unclear billing policies create friction and erode trust. When developers can accurately predict what they'll pay and what they'll get, they're far more comfortable committing to your platform.

Measure business success through developer achievement. When your customers succeed, you succeed. This isn't just feel-good philosophy, it's sustainable business strategy. Developers who build successful products on your platform become your best case studies, your most effective advocates, and often your largest accounts.

Key takeaways

DevRel promotes healthy usage, not sales. DevRel drives revenue indirectly through developer success, community building, and removing friction, never through quotas or sales metrics.

Monetization models shape DevRel tactics. Freemium, usage-based, subscription, and open-source models each require different approaches to value exchange.

Clear boundaries with sales. DevRel opens doors and proves value. Sales closes deals. Mixing these roles damages both functions.

Trust is non-negotiable. Community trust is DevRel's most valuable asset. Protect it by prioritizing developer success over short-term revenue.

Healthy usage drives sustainable growth. Promote efficient, value-driven usage patterns that benefit developers, not wasteful consumption that benefits only the bottom line.

In 👉 **Chapter 8**, we'll show how to measure and prove the impact of these activities through metrics that matter to both developers and the business.

EIGHT

Feedback and Measurement: How to Learn and What to Track

WHAT GETS MEASURED GETS FUNDED.

Executing a framework without a feedback loop is useless. Chapters 1-7 gave you the strategies and tactics to build a developer ecosystem, but implementation alone doesn't guarantee success. You need to experiment with different approaches, measure what's actually working, learn from both successes and failures, and continuously improve. This chapter shows you how to close that loop, how to know whether your onboarding is actually removing friction, whether your community programs are creating advocates, and whether your monetization strategy is sustainable. Without measurement, you're flying blind. With it, you're building a learning system that gets better over time.

Metrics turn hunches into evidence. Evidence earns resources. Use 👉 **Chapter 1** to choose one ICP and one North Star, Chapters 3-7 to ship tactics, and this chapter to prove what moved. When the dashboard goes red, start here, not in your opinions.

Why measurement matters

> "Everyone has an idea of what a great onboarding experience looks like, but opinions don't matter when you've got good data. If you have 1,000 people a day signing up and 10 people completing onboarding, you have a problem."
>
> Jim Bennett (Principal Developer Experience Engineer, Arize AI)

Developer-facing products live or die by the trust they inspire. Yet many teams still treat DevRel as a feel-good function judged by conference applause or social media likes. That's the fastest route to a budget cut. Measurement turns hunches into evidence, and evidence wins resources.

Four hard truths make measurement non-negotiable:

Perception doesn't equal reality. A lively Discord may hide silent churn if newcomers never reach production use. Metrics expose the gap between excitement and sustained value.

Success without proof is luck. If you can't demonstrate which guide or SDK revision made the difference, every roadmap debate becomes opinion versus opinion. Data lets you double down on what works and sunset what doesn't.

Executives speak ARR, not anecdotes. When budgets are tightened, initiatives with a clear line to revenue tend to survive. Activation rate, expansion ARR, and developer-sourced pipeline translate DevRel outcomes into language the C-suite respects.

Staying relevant means connecting to company goals. Show how your work ties to what leadership cares about most, even indirectly. At Slack, 97% of paying customers used the platform's API. That didn't mean Slack charged for API access, but it definitely meant DevRel made paying customers happy, and customer happiness was a top company goal. Find your version of that connection.

Measurement also changes culture. Once teams see weekly dashboards, they stop shipping docs "just to ship" and start asking, "What friction will this remove?" Engineers embed analytics hooks by default, advocates design tutorials around measurable aha moments, and product managers prioritize features that unblock activation over vanity integrations.

Measure to accelerate developer success, not to justify DevRel's existence.

Metric categories at a glance

To avoid metric overload, group every data point under four pillars. Each pillar answers a distinct business question.

Reach

Are we on developers' radars? Think docs visits, GitHub stars, newsletter opens. Reach metrics matter only as leading indicators. They foreshadow funnel volume but never guarantee activation.

Activation

Do new developers achieve real value? Core signals include time-to-first-production call, percentage of signups that send real data, and first webhook fired. Activation is the first point where usage correlates strongly with future revenue.

Retention and engagement

Do developers stick around and deepen usage? Track feature breadth, weekly active tokens, number of teammates invited, or SDK update adoption. Healthy retention converts activation spikes into a stable user base and community advocates.

Revenue alignment

Does developer activity translate to dollars and pipeline? Monitor self-serve upgrade rate, expansion ARR from developer-led accounts, and developer-sourced sales opportunities. These metrics tie DevRel success to the company's P&L statement.

Avoid the temptation to measure everything from Day One. Start with one North Star metric per pillar, ensure data quality, then layer detail as your analytics maturity grows.

Choose your leading plus lagging indicators by stage

A healthy DevRel measurement stack strikes a balance. Rely on lagging indicators alone, and you'll learn about problems only after they've already hurt adoption or revenue. Rely on leading indicators alone, you'll optimize for activity that never materializes into value.

Pick one leading and one lagging metric per stage. Leading predicts what to fix now; lagging confirms success later.

Awareness: Docs to quickstart CTR (leading), branded search volume (lagging)

Onboarding: Quickstart completion rate (leading), median time to first real call (lagging)

Activation: Real-call success within 24 hours (leading), seven-day retention for activated users (lagging)

Engagement: Community answer rate under 24 hours (leading), feature breadth per account (lagging)

Monetization: Upgrade intent from activated users (leading), expansion ARR from dev-led accounts (lagging)

The balance principle

A leading metric without a lagging counterpart breeds vanity. High newsletter clicks but no activations? Your content title is clickbait.

A lagging metric without a leading counterpart makes you reactive. Churn is up, too late; those developers are gone.

Pairing metrics forces you to answer "Are we on track?" and "Did we succeed?"

Mapping metrics to the developer funnel

Below you'll find a narrative walkthrough of how to choose one leading and one lagging metric for each stage.

Awareness: put the right developers in front of the right story

Leading: Docs to quickstart click-through rate (CTR). A spike here means your content is resonating.

Lagging: Branded search volume. If developers remember your name a month later, awareness is sticking.

Why it works: A flashy tweet may drive traffic, but only a motivated click into the quickstart predicts genuine intent.

Onboarding: convert curiosity into a credible Hello World moment

Leading: Quickstart completion rate. Signals whether guides and SDKs are friction-free.

Lagging: Median time to first real call (TTFA). Confirms how long it takes to produce value.

Key point: Completion alone isn't enough; speed matters. A 45-minute quickstart tutorial is a misnomer.

Activation: help developers solve a real problem with real data

Leading: Percentage of signups who call the API with custom payloads within 24 hours.

Lagging: Seven-day activation retention. If they come back after a week, the value has stuck.

Tip: Count a "first success" only when real data flows on a production key.

Engagement: deepen usage and foster community momentum

Leading: Community answer rate under 24 hours. A vibrant peer network predicts stickiness.

Lagging: Feature breadth per account. More endpoints or SDK modules equal higher switching cost and better retention.

Watch out: Engagement that's 100% staff-driven is a facade. Healthy communities are self-sustaining.

Monetization: translate technical value into commercial value

Leading: Pricing page views or upgrade clicks by activated developers. Early intent shows readiness to pay.

Lagging: Expansion ARR from developer-sourced accounts. The ultimate proof of developer-led growth.

Balance: Aggressive paywalls may spike revenue but crush activation. Pair revenue metrics with activation health to avoid short-term wins that hurt long-term adoption.

Vanity metrics versus growth metrics

Vanity metrics feel good because they rise quickly and look impressive on a slide deck. Unfortunately, they rarely correlate with developer success or revenue and often mask deeper problems.

Why vanity metrics persist

They're easy to collect. Web analytics spits out total page views by default, so teams report them without asking, "What does this prove?"

They feel intuitive. More Twitter followers must mean more awareness, right? Not if 80% are bots or colleagues.

They offer quick wins. Buying conference swag guarantees badge scans; running a bot can generate GitHub stars. Real adoption takes longer.

They're rarely challenged. When dashboards glow green, nobody asks uncomfortable questions, until churn spikes.

Common vanity metrics to retire

- **Total page views** → Track unique docs visitors to quickstart CTR instead
- **Twitter/X followers** → Track click-throughs from social to docs and activation percentage
- **Conference booth scans** → Track post-event signups to first real API call
- **GitHub watchers** → Track pull-request contributors or issue commenters
- **Newsletter subscribers** → Track open plus click to quickstart CTR
- **Discord/Slack member count** → Track community answer rate (peer answers in under 24 hours)

If doubling a metric wouldn't change your next sprint, remove it from the main dashboard.

Qualitative signals from community and support

Numbers alone don't capture community health. You can have perfect activation rates while your community slowly turns toxic, or declining metrics while building genuine loyalty. Regular assessment of community sentiment provides essential insights that dashboards miss.

Pay attention to the tone of discussions. Monitor whether conversations trend toward complaints or praise, problem-solving or venting. A community that's frustrated with your product will show it in how developers talk to each other long before it shows up in churn metrics.

Run regular surveys asking specific questions about pain points, what they wish existed, and what almost made them quit. The answers often surprise you.

Watch behavioral patterns closely. Do experienced developers help newcomers, or do questions go unanswered? How do people handle disagreements, constructively or by attacking? These patterns reveal whether you've built a healthy culture or just accumulated users.

Support ticket analysis reveals patterns that point to deeper issues. When multiple developers hit the same confusion point, that's not a support problem, it's a documentation gap or product issue. Track ticket themes, not just volume. The questions developers ask repeatedly tell you exactly where your onboarding is failing.

Conduct regular conversations with developers at different stages. User interviews reveal insights metrics can't capture. A churned developer might explain they hit a specific error that your metrics just show as "dropped off at step 3."

The goal isn't to replace quantitative measurement with qualitative feedback, it's to use both. Numbers show what's happening. Conversations reveal why. Combined, they give you the complete picture you need to actually improve.

DevRel reporting to leadership

Translating developer success into business outcomes requires clear, compelling reporting that speaks the language of executives.

What executives care about

Impact to top goals. Connect DevRel to whatever leadership cares about most. For revenue-focused companies, show how DevRel influences trial-to-paid conversion, expansion revenue, and customer retention. For retention-focused companies, highlight how developers using your API stick around longer. For growth-stage companies, demonstrate market share gains or competitive wins. The key is aligning to the company's actual priorities, not a generic list of metrics.

Pipeline contribution. What percentage of sales opportunities originated from developer activity or DevRel touchpoints?

Product feedback and improvement. How has DevRel surfaced critical product issues, validated feature priorities, or prevented costly mistakes? Executives value teams that help the company build the right things.

Efficiency gains. How has DevRel reduced support costs, improved activation rates, or accelerated time-to-value?

Competitive position. How does your developer experience compare to competitors? What's your NPS trend?

Effective reporting cadence

Weekly: Internal team review of leading indicators and immediate action items **Monthly:** Cross-functional review of funnel health and friction points **Quarterly:** Executive business review connecting DevRel metrics to business outcomes **Annually:** Strategic planning linking DevRel initiatives to company OKRs

Dashboard design principles

One screen, five tiles. Each stage gets one tile with a traffic light threshold **Leading plus lagging pairs.** Show both current trajectory and validated outcomes **Drill-down links.** Executives see summary; practitioners click through for detail **Alert thresholds.** Red metrics trigger automated investigation workflows.

Key takeaways

Measurement drives improvement. You can't improve what you don't measure. Track metrics that guide decisions, not just justify budgets.

Pair leading and lagging metrics. Leading indicators predict problems; lagging indicators prove success. You need both.

Vanity metrics mask reality. Total followers, page views, and event attendance don't predict business outcomes. Focus on activation, retention, and revenue alignment.

Stage-specific metrics matter. Different funnel stages need different measurements. Don't conflate awareness metrics with activation metrics.

Qualitative insights complete the picture. Numbers show what's happening; conversations reveal why. Combine both for complete understanding.

Executive reporting connects dots. Show how DevRel metrics link to business outcomes. Speak in terms of revenue, efficiency, and competitive advantage.

Now that you know what to measure and how to measure it, ☞ **Chapter 9** will help you understand what DevRel is at a deeper level and how to justify and grow your DevRel investment within your organization.

NINE

What Is Developer Relations and Why It Matters

UNDERSTAND WHAT DEVREL IS REALLY ABOUT, CREATING VALUE FOR DEVELOPERS THAT DRIVES VALUE FOR THE BUSINESS.

Up until now, we've focused entirely on the framework, how to build and scale your developer ecosystem from zero to hero. You've learned the strategy, the tactics, and the measurement systems needed to drive developer adoption and success. If that's all you needed to know, this is a great place to pause. Consider leaving a positive review or sharing this book with someone who needs it.

But if you're interested in how to build a Developer Relations (DevRel) organization that can successfully execute this framework, how to hire the right team, position DevRel strategically, justify ongoing investment, and ensure DevRel has the organizational support it needs to succeed, then keep reading. The remaining chapters shift from "what to do" to "how to organize and scale the team that does it."

What is Developer Relations (beyond swag and demos)

Developer Relations often gets reduced to conference talks, swag distribution, and friendly faces at hackathons. But this surface-level view misses the strategic core of what makes DevRel valuable. At its heart, Developer Relations is about creating sustainable, mutually beneficial relationships between your company and the developers who use (or could use) your products.

DevRel is not marketing. While DevRel activities may create awareness, the primary goal isn't to generate leads or drive campaigns. DevRel focuses on enabling developer success through education, community building, and advocacy. The value it creates is indirect but powerful.

DevRel is not sales. DevRel teams should never carry quotas or be measured on closed deals. The moment DevRel becomes a sales function, it loses its most valuable asset: developer trust. Developers can smell inauthenticity from miles away, and once trust is broken, it's nearly impossible to rebuild.

DevRel is not technical support. While DevRel professionals often help developers solve problems, their role extends far beyond answering support tickets. They identify patterns in developer struggles, advocate for product improvements, and create resources that prevent issues before they occur. Note: Sometimes Developer Support organizationally reports to DevRel, and that's fine, but make sure DevRel itself has a strategic seat in your organization, not just a tactical support function.

So what is DevRel? It's the function that ensures your product creates value for developers while driving value for your business. DevRel sits at the intersection of product, marketing, sales, and support, serving as a bridge between your company and the developer community. It's measured by developer success, not just business metrics.

> "The nature of your job is very two-headed. You are the voice of Slack to our global developer community. That is a full-time job. And then you are also the face of that developer community back inside of Slack, also a very full-time job. And so you have to figure out how to balance those things."
>
> Jim Ray (Director, Developer Advocacy, Slack, Bluesky)

"Developers drive technology adoption. Their trust and endorsement forecast market share better than traditional analyst quadrants."

Common Developer Relations roles

Developer Relations organizations can include many different roles depending on company size and needs. Here are some of the most common:

Developer Advocate is the classical DevRel role focused on advocacy of an API or platform. These are the people you see online or on stage giving technical presentations at conferences. They create content, speak at events, engage with the developer community, and serve as the public face of your developer platform. Core skills include great communication abilities, strong interpersonal skills, and high technical proficiency. They need to code well enough to be credible but excel at explaining complex concepts clearly.

Developer Relations Engineer (sometimes called DevExp Engineer) is all about code. These team members build SDKs, create sample code, develop the developer portal and onboarding experience, contribute to open source projects, and handle code integration with top partners. Core skills are software engineering combined with technical writing. They're often former or current engineers who enjoy building tools that help other developers succeed rather than building end-user products directly.

Developer Relations Program Manager is a diverse role that can mean anything from managing your beta program to serving as a regional lead for DevRel in a specific geography (like Japan, for example). Some program managers focus on events and hackathons, others on partner programs or certification initiatives. Core skills require the ability to manage complex projects and drive results for a given program or region. They're the operational backbone that turns DevRel strategy into executed programs.

Developer Relations Community Manager is a specialized subset of program management focused on fostering communities of developers around your platform. This might mean managing online forums, organizing meetups, running ambassador programs, or moderating Discord servers. The core skill is the ability to enlist and activate communities at scale, identifying natural leaders, creating programs that empower them, and maintaining healthy community culture as it grows.

Your first DevRel hire might wear all these hats. As you scale, you'll likely specialize into distinct roles based on your specific needs and growth stage.

When to hire your first DevRel

The timing of your first DevRel hire matters immensely. Hire too early, and you'll waste resources trying to polish a product that isn't ready. Hire too late, and you'll struggle to build momentum in an increasingly crowded marketplace.

Before hiring dedicated DevRel, founders and product leaders often fill this role. Many successful companies started with technical founders or product leaders acting as their first developer advocates. Android product leaders were also amazing DevRel professionals who deeply understood both the product and the developer community. Startup CEOs like those at Daytona and Kong are fantastic advocates for their products, speaking at conferences, engaging with developers, and building community. This founder-led DevRel can be highly effective in the early days, just recognize when it's time to bring in dedicated expertise so leadership can focus on other priorities.

> "The only way for it to be authentic is if the founder is doing it. When you have a hire, they speak under the tone of voice set by the company. The only people that can set it are the founders. When the founder says something, it's more authentic and carries much more weight."
>
> Ivan Burazin (Founder, Daytona)

Signs you're ready for DevRel

You have product-market fit with at least one developer segment. This doesn't mean your product is perfect, but it does mean some developers are successfully using it to solve real problems. If you're still figuring out what to build or pivoting frequently, you're not ready for DevRel.

Your documentation exists but could be better. You need baseline documentation before hiring DevRel. Your first DevRel hire shouldn't be creating docs from scratch. They should be improving them, finding gaps, and helping developers succeed faster.

You're getting repeat questions that suggest systemic issues. When support tickets, forum posts, and GitHub issues show patterns, you need someone to turn those insights into better resources, clearer documentation, or product improvements.

You have a way to measure developer success. Before hiring DevRel, you need basic instrumentation: API calls, signup flows, error rates, and activation metrics. DevRel needs data to know what's working and what isn't.

You're ready to listen and act on feedback. DevRel only works if the company is willing to make changes based on developer needs. If your product team isn't ready to hear and act on feedback, DevRel will be frustrated and ineffective.

Signs you're not ready

You don't have working SDKs or APIs yet. DevRel can't advocate for a product that doesn't exist or doesn't work.

Your product changes weekly with breaking changes. Developers need stability. Constant breaking changes make it impossible to build a community or create lasting content.

**You think DevRel's job is to make developers like a bad

product. No amount of charm or swag can overcome poor developer experience. Fix the product first.

You can't afford to invest in developer success without immediate ROI. DevRel is a long-term investment. If you need results this quarter, focus on sales and marketing instead.

DevRel as part of the product organization

One of the most critical decisions for a new DevRel function is where it sits in the organization. While there's no single right answer, the most successful DevRel teams often report into product rather than marketing or sales.

Why product alignment matters

Credibility and trust. When DevRel reports to product, it signals that developer feedback directly influences what gets built. This alignment creates credibility with the developer community because they see their input leading to real changes.

Faster feedback loops. Product-aligned DevRel can escalate developer pain points and feature requests directly to the teams who can address them. There's no translation layer or competing priorities from other departments.

Holistic developer experience. The best developer experiences result from product decisions, not just documentation or tutorials. When DevRel sits in product, they can influence API design, SDK quality, error messages, and other core experience elements.

Protected from short-term revenue pressure. Marketing and sales teams are often measured on quarterly goals that can create pressure for DevRel to behave more like lead generation or sales. Product alignment protects DevRel from these pressures.

> "I've always valued the fact that developer relations at Slack is seated within the product org. I'm not going to say that there's one right way to do it, but I think particularly at an organization that is so product focused, it was such a key signal from the very earliest days. Hey, we're going to put DevRel inside of product."
>
> Jim Ray (Director, Developer Advocacy, Slack, Bluesky)

Alternative models

That said, DevRel can work in other structures:

Marketing alignment works when your product is well-established and the primary goal is awareness and adoption. The risk is that DevRel becomes too focused on campaigns and not enough on genuine developer success.

Independent DevRel reporting to the CEO or a dedicated executive can work in companies where developer experience is core to the business model. This structure works best when the company is large enough to support a standalone function.

Split model where different DevRel functions report to different departments (for example, advocacy to marketing, technical enablement to product) can work but requires excellent communication to avoid conflicts.

The key is ensuring DevRel has the authority and resources to advocate for developers and influence the product experience, regardless of where it sits on the org chart.

How to justify the investment in DevRel

Getting budget and headcount for DevRel requires demonstrating value in language executives understand. While DevRel's impact is often indirect, it can and should be measured.

The business case for DevRel

When justifying DevRel investment to leadership, connect it to metrics they already care about. Here's how DevRel drives business value:

Organic adoption through word of mouth, content, and community is far cheaper than paid advertising. DevRel creates the conditions for natural growth, dramatically reducing your acquisition costs. Instead of spending thousands per developer on ads, you're building content and community that attracts developers at a fraction of the cost.

Better documentation, samples, and support help developers succeed faster, which means more trial users convert to paying customers. This faster time to value directly impacts revenue. When developers can go from signup to their first successful integration in minutes instead of hours or days, conversion rates climb.

Developers who feel supported, heard, and successful stick around. DevRel's community-building efforts create switching costs beyond just technical integration. A developer who's built relationships in your community, contributed to discussions, and gotten help when stuck won't easily abandon that for a competitor.

DevRel identifies friction points and feature gaps before they become widespread problems. This product improvement feedback helps your team build what developers actually need rather than what you think they need. The intelligence DevRel gathers from talking to hundreds of developers is invaluable for product direction.

In platform businesses, DevRel helps grow the ecosystem of integrations, extensions, and third-party tools that make your platform more valuable to everyone. This ecosystem growth creates network effects that compound over time.

Metrics that matter

For your initial DevRel business case, focus on metrics that connect directly to business outcomes. Here are some common examples, choose the ones most relevant to your business model and adapt as needed:

Track your developer activation rate, what percentage of signups become active users? DevRel should improve this metric through better onboarding and education. A jump from 20% to 30% activation means 50% more developers actually using your platform from the same signup volume.

Measure time to first value: how long from signup to first successful use? This metric captures the quality of your developer experience in a single number. Every hour you shave off this time increases conversion rates.

Net Promoter Score (NPS) predicts word-of-mouth growth. When developers enthusiastically recommend your platform to others, your organic growth accelerates. NPS gives you a leading indicator of whether that's happening.

Community activity matters, but focus on genuine engagement rather than vanity metrics. Questions answered, content shared, and events attended indicate real community health. Total follower counts mean nothing if those followers aren't actively engaged.

Track influenced revenue by identifying developers who engaged with DevRel resources before becoming customers. This attribution isn't perfect, but it demonstrates impact. When you can show that 60% of new paying customers engaged with your documentation or attended your webinars first, you're building a clear connection between DevRel and revenue.

The 90-day plan

When proposing DevRel investment, include a clear 90-day plan that shows early wins. Here's an example framework, adapt the specific activities to match your business context and priorities:

First 30 days:

- Audit existing documentation and identify top gaps
- Instrument basic developer funnel metrics
- Identify your top 5 developer pain points through support analysis
- Create or improve one critical piece of developer content

Days 31-60:

- Launch or improve one developer community channel (forum, Discord, etc.)
- Run first developer event or office hours
- Ship improvements to onboarding based on early findings
- Establish regular feedback loop with product team

Days 61-90:

- Present data on improved metrics
- Showcase early community wins and testimonials
- Propose expanded programs based on what's working
- Demonstrate clear pipeline from developer engagement to business value

The goal is to show quick wins that justify continued investment while building the foundation for long-term programs. Customize this timeline based on your organization's pace and what will resonate most with your leadership team.

The maturity model

Most DevRel programs progress through these maturity levels:

Reactive (0-6 months). You're responding to immediate fires, setting up baseline infrastructure, and figuring out priorities. Focus: Get onboarding working and activation measurable.

Programmatic (6-18 months). You have repeatable processes for common activities, clear metrics, and can run programs predictably. Focus: Scale what works and eliminate what doesn't.

Strategic (18-36 months). You influence product roadmap, align with business OKRs, and demonstrate clear ROI. DevRel is recognized as a growth driver. Focus: Cross-functional integration and ecosystem development.

Transformational (36+ months). Developer experience is a competitive differentiator, community is self-sustaining, and DevRel informs company strategy. Focus: Industry leadership and ecosystem innovation.

Progress isn't automatic. You can stay reactive for years if you don't build systems, or regress if you lose focus on fundamentals.

Common DevRel misconceptions

Before we wrap up this chapter, let's address some critical misconceptions about DevRel metrics that can derail even well-intentioned programs.

DevRel can't fix product-market fit problems. If your product hasn't reached product-market fit, everything Developer Relations does will struggle to show impact. DevRel is downstream of a great product or service. You can have the most talented advocates, the best documentation, and thriving community programs, but if developers don't fundamentally want what you're building, DevRel won't save you. Fix the product first. DevRel amplifies what's already working, it can't create something from nothing.

DevRel takes time to show results. Developer adoption cycles are measured in quarters, not weeks. Wait at least one quarter, preferably six months, before judging DevRel progress and effectiveness. Developer trust builds slowly through consistent, authentic engagement over time. Early wins like improved documentation or initial community formation are important milestones, but the real impact, increased activation rates, stronger retention, meaningful revenue influence, takes longer to materialize. Patience is essential, especially in the early stages.

Involve DevRel early in the feature lifecycle. Don't hand DevRel a finished feature and expect them to magically drive adoption. Involve them early so they can set strategy, plan content and programs, gather early feedback from beta users, and ensure the developer experience is considered from the start.

When DevRel is brought in at the last minute, they're forced into reactive mode rather than strategic planning. Early involvement leads to better launches and stronger adoption.

Don't become obsessed with metrics. Yes, measurement matters, we dedicated an entire chapter to it. But make sure DevRel, and more generally your entire organization, doesn't become so obsessed with metrics that you lose flexibility and creativity. Plans change. Markets shift. Developer needs evolve. Enable your team to adapt and experiment. Sometimes the most valuable DevRel activities don't fit neatly into dashboards. Trust your team's judgment alongside the data.

Some things are hard to measure but still critical. Brand awareness and developer trust are notoriously difficult to quantify, yet they're among DevRel's most important contributions. You can track proxies like NPS or social mentions, but these metrics don't fully capture the value of being a trusted voice in the developer community or having a strong reputation that precedes you. Don't dismiss these intangible benefits just because they're hard to measure. Recognize that not everything that matters can be easily quantified.

Key takeaways

DevRel is strategic, not tactical. It's not about swag and demos, it's about creating sustainable value for both developers and your business through education, community, and advocacy.

Timing matters. Don't hire DevRel too early or too late. Wait until you have product-market fit, basic documentation, and the organizational readiness to act on developer feedback.

Organizational placement shapes effectiveness. Where DevRel sits in your org chart matters. Product alignment often works best because it gives DevRel the influence to improve the developer experience holistically.

Measure what matters. DevRel should be measured on developer success metrics (activation, time to value, NPS) rather than sales metrics (quotas, deals closed). These leading indicators predict business outcomes.

DevRel maturity is a journey. Most programs progress from reactive to programmatic to strategic to transformational over 3+ years. Understanding where you are helps set realistic expectations.

Start with quick wins. A clear 90-day plan with measurable improvements helps justify the investment and builds momentum for longer-term programs.

Now that you understand what DevRel is, how to justify the investment, and where it should sit organizationally, ☞ **Chapter 10** explores how to build effective cross-functional partnerships that multiply your impact across product, marketing, sales, and beyond.

TEN

DevRel as the Bridge: Cross-Functional Collaboration

DEVREL DOESN'T WORK IN ISOLATION, IT'S THE BRIDGE.

DevRel sits at the intersection of product, marketing, sales, and support. The most effective DevRel teams don't just build developer relationships, they serve as bridges between developers and every function inside the company. This chapter explores how to build productive cross-functional relationships that multiply DevRel's impact.

Product: early feedback, internal dogfooding

The relationship between DevRel and Product is perhaps the most critical for developer success. DevRel sees patterns across thousands of developer interactions while Product has the power to fix systemic issues. When these two functions collaborate effectively, you create a powerful feedback loop that continuously improves the developer experience.

Creating effective feedback loops

Every support interaction, community conversation, and user interview is a learning opportunity. But raw feedback without structure is just noise. Create systems to tag, categorize, and analyze patterns so you can surface meaningful insights rather than random complaints.

Schedule weekly friction reviews where DevRel presents the top developer pain points with specific examples and reproduction steps. Don't just say "developers find authentication confusing", show the exact error messages they're hitting, the documentation they're reading, and where they're getting stuck. Product teams need concrete, actionable information.

Not every piece of feedback warrants immediate action. Help product teams prioritize based on frequency, severity, and strategic alignment. If three developers complain about a niche edge case, that's different from hundreds hitting the same onboarding wall. Use data to guide these conversations.

When product ships improvements based on community feedback, announce it publicly. Close the loop. This demonstrates that developer voices actually matter and encourages future participation. Developers who see their feedback implemented become your strongest advocates.

> "If you have a breaking change or something that you know is going to break everything or ruin something for your developer ecosystem, give them a heads up early. They've all been around for a long time, so they understand that things on the internet and in software have to get changed. You really need to make sure that you give them at least four to five months heads up."
>
> Cecilia Stallsmith (Head of Marketing, Lovable)

Internal dogfooding

DevRel teams should use the product extensively and document every stumble. You're in a unique position to experience your own product with both technical expertise and fresh eyes.

New DevRel hires are gold mines for this. They experience your product with fresh eyes before they've learned to work around all the rough edges. Capture their struggles and questions during onboarding. What confused them? Where did they get stuck? These insights reveal blind spots your veteran team has normalized.

Periodically attempt common integration patterns and document friction points. Don't just build the happy path, try the scenarios developers actually encounter. What happens when auth tokens expire? How do you handle rate limiting? Where does error handling fall apart?

Regularly show engineering teams real developer workflows to build empathy. When engineers see actual developers struggling with something they thought was obvious, it creates motivation to fix it. Live demos of real integration attempts are far more powerful than feature requests in a ticket.

Marketing: campaigns, content strategy, SEO

DevRel and Marketing often overlap in content creation and developer outreach, but their goals and approaches differ. Marketing optimizes for reach and leads; DevRel optimizes for activation and trust. Clear collaboration prevents conflicts and multiplies reach.

Content collaboration

Coordinate timing through a shared content calendar to avoid conflicts and create mutual amplification opportunities. When Marketing launches a campaign and DevRel publishes complementary technical content the same week, both perform better. When they compete for attention, both suffer.

Marketing focuses on awareness, getting developers interested. DevRel focuses on activation and retention, getting developers successful. Both are necessary, and they work best when they're explicitly coordinated rather than accidentally overlapping or competing.

Marketing brings SEO expertise that DevRel often lacks. DevRel brings technical credibility that marketing struggles to fake. Combine both for developer-focused content that ranks well and actually helps developers. The best content answers real technical questions while also being discoverable.

Marketing content can feel too polished for developers. All the professional photography, perfect formatting, and sales-y language triggers developer skepticism. DevRel ensures technical accuracy and maintains the authentic developer voice that makes content trustworthy. Sometimes "good enough" documentation beats perfectly designed marketing pages.

Campaign alignment

When Marketing runs campaigns, DevRel ensures they link to quickstarts and working code, not just landing pages and signup forms. Developers want to see the product in action, not read about how great it is. If your campaign can't deliver immediate technical value, it won't resonate with developers.

Coordinate conference presence, webinars, and community events to maximize impact. One team shouldn't be running a webinar the same day the other is hosting a major conference session. Stack your efforts strategically.

Help Marketing understand that 100 activated developers beat 10,000 unqualified signups. Marketing often optimizes for volume because that's what they're measured on. DevRel helps shift focus to quality metrics that actually predict business outcomes.

Sales: field engineering and enablement

Sales wants to close deals; DevRel wants to enable developer success. These goals align when properly structured, but they conflict when DevRel gets treated as pre-sales engineering.

Sales enablement

DevRel can help sales understand developer technical requirements and evaluate fit during discovery calls. When sales brings DevRel into technical discovery conversations, they close more deals because they're qualifying better and setting accurate expectations. This is support, not selling.

Help prospects succeed with technical proof-of-concepts without making DevRel the delivery team. Your job is to teach them to fish, not to fish for them. Provide guidance, documentation, and troubleshooting, but the prospect should be driving their own PoC implementation.

Create reusable demos that sales can confidently present without deep technical expertise. Sales reps shouldn't need to be senior engineers to show your product. Build demo environments, scripts, and talking points that work reliably.

Arm sales with responses to common technical objections based on real developer conversations. When prospects ask "how do you handle X," sales should have credible answers drawn from actual developer experiences rather than making things up.

Handoff protocols

Define when a developer is truly sales-ready. Active usage matters. Production deployment matters. Team adoption matters. A single developer who ran "hello world" once is not a qualified sales opportunity, no matter what their company size is.

Ensure sales has context from DevRel interactions without violating developer trust. If a developer has been active in your community, sales should know about it. But if a developer explicitly said they're just exploring options, sales shouldn't call them with a pitch. Information sharing requires judgment and boundaries.

Create feedback loops where sales learns why technical deals are lost and DevRel addresses common friction points. When enterprise deals die because your enterprise features are incomplete, that's product feedback. When they die because prospects can't get through onboarding, that's a DevRel problem to solve.

Partnerships: SI and channel plays

Strategic partnerships can dramatically extend DevRel's reach when properly structured. The right partners multiply your impact without multiplying your headcount.

System integrator relationships

Train partner engineers on your platform through enablement programs so they can deliver customer implementations. System integrators need to be as proficient with your platform as your own team. Create certification programs, training materials, and ongoing support.

Joint webinars, case studies, and content that showcase integrations create co-marketing opportunities that benefit both companies. When you and your SI partner tell a customer success story together, you're reaching both audiences with shared credibility.

Provide partners with dedicated support channels for customer engagements. When an SI is implementing your platform for a major customer, they need faster response times than community support provides. Partner support demonstrates that you're invested in their success.

Technology partnerships

Work with complementary platforms to create official integrations that benefit both communities. A great integration with a popular tool brings their users to your platform and your users to their tool. Everybody wins.

Coordinate launches, content, and events with technology partners for joint go-to-market initiatives. When you launch an integration, do it together with coordinated announcements, blog posts, and demonstrations. Double the amplification.

Each integration expands your addressable market and provides more value to existing users. The more your platform integrates with tools developers already use, the more valuable you become to everyone. Developer ecosystem growth compounds.

Aligning DevRel to the C-suite

DevRel must speak the language of executives to secure resources and maintain strategic alignment. Developers care about code quality and API design. Executives care about revenue and competitive advantage. Your job is to translate between these worlds.

Connecting DevRel to business outcomes

Show how DevRel touchpoints correlate with conversion, expansion, and retention through revenue influence tracking. When you can demonstrate that developers who attended your webinar are 40% more likely to convert to paid plans, you're speaking executive language.

Demonstrate how better documentation reduces support costs and improves activation rates through efficiency metrics. Executives love anything that reduces cost or improves conversion. Frame DevRel wins in these terms.

Report on developer sentiment about your platform versus competitors. Competitive intelligence matters at the executive level. When you can show that your developer NPS is climbing while competitors are struggling, that's strategic information.

Connect DevRel activities to company OKRs and strategic priorities. If the company's top priority is enterprise growth, show how DevRel is enabling enterprise adoption. If it's international expansion, highlight regional community building. Align your narrative to existing priorities.

Executive communication

Present DevRel impact in quarterly business reviews using terms executives understand: revenue influence, pipeline contribution, competitive position. Don't lead with community engagement metrics. Lead with business outcomes, then explain how community drove those outcomes.

Provide brief monthly health reports with updates on key metrics, significant wins, and emerging concerns. Executives don't need to know everything, but they should never be surprised. Flag problems early.

Participate in company planning to ensure developer experience is considered in product strategy. When the company is setting annual goals, DevRel should have input to ensure developer success is represented in strategic planning, not just tactical execution.

Key takeaways

DevRel is a bridge, not an island. Maximum impact comes from effective collaboration across product, marketing, sales, and partnerships.

Product partnership is critical. DevRel surfaces patterns; Product fixes systemic issues. Both are necessary for sustainable developer success.

Marketing amplifies reach. Clear collaboration prevents conflicts and ensures developer-focused content reaches the right audiences.

Sales needs enablement, not quotas. DevRel supports sales success through enablement and qualification, not by carrying quotas.

Partnerships multiply impact. Strategic technology and SI partnerships extend reach and add value to existing developers.

Executive alignment secures resources. Demonstrate business impact in terms executives understand: revenue, efficiency, competitive advantage.

Cross-functional collaboration isn't just good politics. It's how DevRel scales impact beyond what a small team could accomplish alone. In **Chapter 11**, we'll explore where developer relations is heading and how to stay ahead of emerging trends.

ELEVEN

The Future of Developer Relations

WHERE IT'S ALL GOING, AND HOW TO STAY AHEAD.

Developer Relations is evolving rapidly, driven by technological advances, changing developer behaviors, and shifts in how companies approach developer experience. This chapter explores emerging trends and how forward-thinking DevRel teams are adapting to stay ahead.

Three tectonic shifts shaping DevRel

The DevRel landscape is being reshaped by three fundamental forces. Understanding these shifts helps you build programs that remain relevant as the industry evolves.

AI everywhere

AI is changing how developers learn and build. Copilots and agents draft code, propose integrations, and query knowledge bases to enhance system functionality. Search transforms into answers. Examples evolve into scaffolds. The boundary between documentation and tools blurs.

What this means for DevRel: Your documentation now serves two audiences, human developers and AI systems that retrieve content on their behalf. Write in short sections with clear titles, stable anchors, and canonical examples. Add metadata including version tags and citations so retrieval works effectively. Treat answers as products: build conversational documentation that cites sources, shows step-by-step processes, and can verify outcomes.

Risks to avoid: Hallucinations erode trust quickly. Stale contexts repeat fixed bugs. Assistants that hide their sources make debugging impossible. Establish evaluation harnesses to test AI assistants like you test SDKs. Publish provenance by stating model versions, data sources, and update timestamps.

First steps: Pick two high-traffic documentation sections and build a small retrieval stack. Expose an assistant alongside the docs and measure answer quality, escalation rate, and whether assistant users activate faster. Expand only when signals are healthy.

> "If you are the one that LLMs recommend, there's so much power in that. It comes down to friction, low friction to the first API call, broad SDK coverage, an up-to-date LLMs.txt. Those are the signals you want AI systems paying attention to."
>
> Zeno Rocha (Co-founder & CEO, Resend)

Agent-based workflows

AI agents that can read documentation, write code, and interact with APIs will fundamentally change how developers evaluate and adopt platforms. This isn't distant future speculation, it's already beginning.

What this means for DevRel: Developer experience will increasingly be judged by how well AI agents can work with your APIs. Clear documentation, consistent patterns, good error messages, and predictable behavior matter even more when agents are attempting automated evaluation and implementation.

Automated evaluation at scale: AI agents could evaluate multiple competing APIs simultaneously, testing functionality, performance, and developer experience without human intervention. Your platform needs to perform well in these automated evaluations or risk being filtered out before human developers even see it.

Self-service becomes mandatory: Agents might complete entire onboarding flows, generate integrations, and optimize implementations without human guidance. Any friction that stops automated progress will eliminate you from consideration.

Strategic decisions remain human: While agents handle tactical implementation, humans still make strategic choices about architecture, tool selection, and system design. DevRel's role shifts toward helping developers make informed strategic decisions rather than just explaining API endpoints.

The transformation is happening faster than many expect. Organizations that embrace AI-assisted development will pull ahead, while those that resist will struggle to keep pace with the accelerating rate of technical change.

> "I found it hilarious that engineers had one of the best jobs, interesting, challenging, all the benefits, and then we engineered ourselves out of our own job. Those who do not adopt AI will not exist in the next five years or will be very much reduced. Those who do adopt AI will pull ahead faster."
>
> Yochay Kiriaty (Director of Product Management, Google Kubernetes Engine)

These three shifts, GenAI everywhere, DevEx as moat, and agent-based workflows, aren't separate trends. They reinforce each other. AI agents rely on excellent DevEx. Strong DevEx increasingly depends on AI assistance. Together, they're raising the bar for what "good" developer relations looks like.

DevRel as a growth engine

Historically, DevRel was often seen as a cost center focused on community engagement and education. Forward-thinking companies now recognize DevRel as a critical growth driver with measurable business impact.

Product-led growth acceleration. DevRel reduces friction in self-serve adoption, directly impacting trial-to-paid conversion.

Developer-led sales. Bottom-up adoption where developers bring tools into enterprises generates more sustainable revenue than top-down sales alone.

Network effects and ecosystem value. Strong developer communities create switching costs and competitive moats that directly impact company valuations.

Customer success at scale. DevRel's content, community, and programs enable developer success without linear scaling of support teams.

The companies winning developer mindshare treat DevRel as a strategic growth function, not a marketing afterthought.

The AI-assisted developer experience

Generative AI has fundamentally changed how developers learn, build, and evaluate tools. Copilots and agents draft code, propose integrations, and query knowledge bases. Search transforms into answers. Examples evolve into scaffolds. The boundary between documentation and tooling increasingly blurs.

This shift amplifies the importance of clarity, trust, and provenance, all areas where Developer Relations naturally excels. Rather than replacing DevRel, AI raises the bar for what great developer experience looks like.

How AI changes developer relations

Write content that machines can understand. Your documentation now serves two audiences: human developers and AI systems that retrieve content on their behalf. Use short sections with clear titles, maintain stable URL anchors, and provide canonical examples. Add metadata including version tags, framework compatibility, and language indicators. When content is well-structured, AI assistants can surface the right answer at the right moment.

Treat answers as products. Build conversational documentation that cites sources, shows step-by-step processes, and can run or verify outcomes. When an AI assistant answers a question, it should always link back to authoritative documentation and provide an escalation route to human support when confidence is low. Developers trust answers more when they can verify the source.

Establish evaluation harnesses. Test your AI assistants the same way you test SDKs. Measure factual accuracy, code correctness, and helpfulness over time. Track drift and regressions when models update or documentation changes. Create a suite of golden prompts with expected outputs and run them after each significant change.

Publish provenance clearly. State which model versions you're using, where training data comes from, and when content was last updated. Be explicit about what is AI-generated versus human-verified versus executable code. Transparency builds trust.

Risks and anti-patterns

Hallucinations erode trust quickly. When AI assistants confidently provide incorrect information, developers lose faith not just in the assistant but in your platform's reliability. Implement guardrails that flag low-confidence answers and require human review for critical workflows.

Stale contexts repeat fixed bugs. If your AI's knowledge base references outdated API parameters or deprecated endpoints, it actively undermines your current documentation. Schedule regular refreshes of training data and implement automated checks that catch version mismatches.

Confidence without citations creates problems. Answers that sound authoritative but conceal their sources make debugging impossible. Always cite and link to source documentation so developers can verify and dive deeper.

Privacy violations have legal consequences. Never train models on user data without explicit consent. Keep sensitive information like API keys and personal data out of both training contexts and logs. One privacy spill can destroy years of trust.

Piloting AI assistants

Start small and measure everything. Pick your two highest-traffic documentation pages and build a retrieval stack that indexes only reviewed, current content. Display an assistant on those pages with clear citations and a prominent "Talk to a human" option.

Track three metrics from day one: answer quality (measured through thumbs up/down and spot checks), escalation rate (how often users need human help), and assistant-assisted activation (whether users who engaged with the assistant activate faster).

Expand only when signals are healthy. If answer quality drops below 80% accuracy or escalation rates exceed 30%, pause expansion and fix the foundation first.

"I'm not convinced that developer relations is going to be completely subsumed and replaced by AI, but I do think that we need to shift and adjust and figure out how we support the tools that our developers are going to use because ultimately that helps us scale. If we can say, here is the MCP server that's going to help you bootstrap your project, that's fantastic for me because it means that my small team that can't talk to every customer now has the tools that the customers can use."

Jim Ray (Director, Developer Advocacy, Slack, Bluesky)

DevEx as product strategy

Developer Experience is increasingly recognized as a product differentiator, not just a nice-to-have.

DX-first product development. Leading companies prioritize developer experience in product decisions, recognizing that superior DX drives adoption even when functionality is similar.

Dedicated DX roles. More companies are creating dedicated Developer Experience roles that bridge product, engineering, and DevRel.

DX measurement becoming standard. Teams track DX metrics (time to first value, activation rates, NPS) as rigorously as product metrics.

Competitive DX analysis. Understanding how your DX compares to competitors informs strategic decisions about where to invest.

DevEx as a moat

Developer experience becomes a competitive advantage when it shortens time to value and reduces cognitive load. Platform engineering and internal portals push product teams to design golden paths. DevRel shifts from broadcast to product partner.

What this means for DevRel: Own the first ten minutes of the developer experience. Quickstarts, SDK ergonomics, and example repositories become a managed backlog with service-level agreements. Treat documentation and samples like products with roadmaps, release cycles, and quality gates.

Close the loop with engineering: Run usability tests on SDKs and consoles. File issues for confusing error messages, poor logging, and authentication friction. Advocate for breaking change policies and versioned deprecations. Bring metrics to planning meetings: time to first activation, Quickstart completion rates, feature adoption breadth, and support deflection numbers become the language of prioritization.

Align with platform engineering: Share friction logs from developers attempting to use your platform. Collaborate on golden paths that provide opinionated starters with authentication, logging, and error handling already configured. Embed DevRel engineers where changes reduce activation time most dramatically.

Decentralized communities

Developer communities are becoming more distributed and autonomous, requiring different engagement approaches.

Discord and specialized platforms. Developers gather in

platform-specific communities (Discord servers, Slack workspaces) rather than forums you control.

Creator economy integration. Developer advocates, educators, and content creators operate independently while amplifying your platform.

Open-source governance models. Successful projects increasingly adopt transparent governance that gives community members real influence.

Token-based incentives. Some communities experiment with tokenomics to reward contributions and align incentives.

The evolving social landscape

Developer communities are migrating to new platforms, and DevRel must follow. The traditional playbook of Twitter, LinkedIn, and blogging is expanding to include platforms where developers increasingly spend their time, even platforms not traditionally associated with technical content.

TikTok and short-form video. While TikTok might seem like an unlikely developer platform, a growing community of developers creates coding tutorials, debugging tips, and tech career advice in 60-second clips. The platform's algorithm surfaces content to interested audiences regardless of follower count, making it viable for reaching developers who prefer visual, fast-paced learning. DevRel teams experimenting with TikTok focus on quick wins, "aha moments," and problem-solving snippets rather than comprehensive tutorials.

The key isn't to replicate documentation on TikTok, it's to spark curiosity that drives developers to your actual resources. A 30-second clip showing a complex problem solved in three lines of code can generate more activation than a perfectly written blog post no one discovers.

Instagram for visual storytelling. Instagram's developer community focuses on visual content: infographics explaining architecture patterns, carousel posts breaking down complex concepts, and behind-the-scenes glimpses of engineering culture. Developer advocates use Instagram Stories for quick tips and polls that drive engagement. While not the primary platform for technical depth, Instagram builds awareness and humanizes your developer brand.

Bluesky and decentralized social. As developers seek alternatives to centralized platforms, Bluesky and similar decentralized networks are attracting technically sophisticated early adopters. DevRel teams that establish presence early on these platforms gain access to influential developers and set norms for how technical communities form there. The developer-friendly nature of Bluesky's AT Protocol makes it particularly appealing to the open-source and privacy-conscious developer segments.

Twitch for live coding and community. Twitch's live-streaming format creates opportunities for real-time engagement that recorded content can't match. Developer advocates stream coding sessions, debug issues live, host office hours where viewers can ask questions in real-time, and run pair programming sessions with community members. The unpolished, authentic nature of live streaming builds trust that perfectly edited YouTube videos sometimes lack.

What makes Twitch powerful for DevRel is the community formation. Regular streams build loyal audiences who return weekly, chat with each other, and form bonds beyond just consuming content. You're not broadcasting to passive viewers, you're building a community that shows up consistently.

The constant migration principle. The specific platforms matter less than the underlying principle: developers move to new platforms constantly, and DevRel must move with them. Five years ago, serious technical discussion happened on Twitter. Today it's fragmenting across Discord servers, Bluesky, niche Slack communities, and platforms we haven't mentioned.

Your job isn't to master every platform that exists. It's to identify where your specific developer audience is active and meet them there with content that fits the platform's format and culture. A TikTok video needs different pacing than a blog post. A Twitch stream requires different preparation than a conference talk.

Platform selection framework. Not every platform deserves your attention. Evaluate platforms based on three criteria:

1. **Audience overlap:** Where does your ICP actually spend time? Don't assume, ask in surveys, check where they share your content, and monitor where technical discussions happen.
2. **Content-platform fit:** Does your message work in this format? Complex architectural decisions don't belong on TikTok. Quick debugging wins do.
3. **Sustainable effort:** Can you maintain consistent presence? Sporadic posting on any platform builds less value than consistent engagement on one platform.

Start with one experimental platform, commit to 90 days of consistent content, measure engagement and activation from that channel, and then decide whether to double down or try something else.

The authenticity requirement. Developers have finely tuned sensors for corporate social media that feels forced. Your Instagram posts shouldn't sound like marketing copy. Your Twitch streams shouldn't be polished product demos. Your TikTok videos shouldn't hide mistakes.

What works on these platforms is the same thing that works everywhere in DevRel: genuine helpfulness. Show up to solve problems, share knowledge, and build relationships, not to hit engagement metrics or drive signups. When you help developers succeed, the business outcomes follow.

Emergent technology domains for DevRel

As technology continues to evolve, several emerging domains present unique opportunities where Developer Relations can play a critical role in accelerating adoption and building sustainable ecosystems.

Robotics

Robotics is transitioning from research labs and industrial settings into broader commercial and consumer applications. This shift creates a massive opportunity for DevRel to bridge hardware and software developers, establish standards, and build communities around robotics platforms.

The robotics developer ecosystem is fragmented across hardware manufacturers, software frameworks (ROS, Isaac, etc.), and application domains (autonomous vehicles, warehouse automation, consumer robots, drones). DevRel teams that can create unified experiences across this fragmentation will have outsized impact.

Unique challenges: Robotics combines hardware constraints, real-time systems, safety considerations, and physical testing requirements that make traditional software developer onboarding insufficient. Developers need access to simulation environments, hardware documentation, safety guidelines, and community support that understands both software and physical systems.

DevRel opportunities: Create comprehensive onboarding that addresses both software SDK usage and hardware integration. Build simulator-first experiences where developers can test without expensive hardware. Foster communities that share best practices for safety, testing, and deployment. Develop certification programs that help developers demonstrate competency in robotics development.

Quantum computing

Quantum computing is moving from theoretical research into practical application development, though still in early stages. This creates a greenfield opportunity for Developer Relations to shape how an entirely new generation of developers learns and adopts quantum programming.

The quantum developer audience is diverse, ranging from physicists and quantum algorithm researchers to classical software engineers exploring quantum applications. DevRel must serve both audiences while making quantum concepts accessible to developers without advanced physics backgrounds.

Unique challenges: Quantum computing requires understanding fundamentally different computational paradigms. Developers need education on quantum mechanics basics, quantum algorithms, and when quantum advantages actually apply. The hardware is still limited, expensive, and accessed primarily through cloud platforms with queue-based systems.

DevRel opportunities: Build educational pathways that gradually introduce quantum concepts through familiar programming patterns. Create simulators and learning environments where developers can experiment without queue times or hardware access. Develop use-case libraries that help developers identify when quantum computing provides genuine advantages over classical approaches. Foster communities where physicists and software engineers learn from each other.

Both robotics and quantum computing represent technology domains where early DevRel investment can establish platforms as category leaders, define standards, and build communities that compound growth over decades.

Emerging skills for DevRel professionals

As DevRel evolves, the skills needed to excel are changing:

Data literacy. Understanding metrics, running experiments, and drawing insights from data become core competencies.

Product thinking. DevRel professionals who understand product strategy and can influence product decisions deliver more impact.

Community platform expertise. Managing Discord, fostering peer-to-peer support, and scaling community programs require specific skills.

AI/ML familiarity. Understanding how developers use AI tools and how AI impacts developer workflows is increasingly important.

Developer tooling creation. Building tools that make developers more productive (linters, CLI tools, IDE extensions) becomes a core DevRel activity.

Key takeaways

DevRel is a growth engine. Forward-thinking companies recognize DevRel as a strategic growth function that directly impacts revenue and competitive position.

AI changes everything. Generative AI transforms how developers discover, learn, and implement solutions. DevRel must adapt while remaining relevant.

Agent-based onboarding is coming. AI agents will evaluate and implement APIs at scale. Make sure your DX works well for both humans and agents.

DX is product strategy. Companies that prioritize developer experience as a product differentiator win developer mindshare and market share.

Communities are decentralizing. Engage developers where they already are rather than forcing them into platforms you control.

Skills are evolving. Data literacy, product thinking, and AI familiarity join technical credibility and communication as core DevRel competencies.

The future of DevRel is exciting and challenging. Teams that embrace these changes while maintaining focus on genuine developer success will thrive. Those that cling to old models risk irrelevance.

Final words

Building successful developer ecosystems is both art and science. It requires technical credibility, authentic relationships, data-driven decision making, and relentless focus on developer success.

The frameworks and tactics in this book provide a foundation, but every developer community is unique. Adapt these principles to your specific context, measure what matters, iterate based on feedback, and never lose sight of why developers choose to invest their time in your platform.

Great DevRel creates value for developers in ways that naturally drive value for the business. It's not about tricks or hacks. It's about genuinely caring about developer success and building systems that scale that care.

Now go build something developers love.

TWELVE

Appendix: Tips & Tools

THIS APPENDIX PROVIDES PRACTICAL RESOURCES, TEMPLATES, AND TACTICAL GUIDANCE TO SUPPORT YOUR DEVREL PRACTICE.

A. Implementation Sprint Plans

This section provides day-by-day implementation plans for teams starting or scaling their DevRel programs. Each sprint includes specific tasks, owners, KPI impacts, and success criteria.

A.1 Foundation Sprint (14 days)

Before launching awareness campaigns or community programs, establish the infrastructure that makes everything else possible. This 14-day sprint creates your baseline developer experience.

Days 1-3: Documentation Foundation

- Task: Audit existing docs, identify top 3 missing pieces
- Owner: Technical writer + Developer advocate
- KPI Impact: Reduces time-to-first-call
- Deliverable: Documentation gap analysis with prioritized backlog

Days 4-6: Quickstart Creation

- Task: Build "Hello World to first API call" guide (< 5 minutes)
- Owner: Developer advocate
- KPI Impact: Activation rate ↑
- Deliverable: Published Quickstart with copy-paste code

Days 7-9: Self-Service Signup

- Task: Implement instant API key generation, remove approval gates
- Owner: Product + DevRel engineer
- KPI Impact: Signup-to-first-call conversion ↑
- Deliverable: Automated key provisioning in < 30 seconds

Days 10-12: Error Messages & Debugging

- Task: Audit top 10 error codes, add actionable guidance
- Owner: Engineering + Technical writer
- KPI Impact: Support ticket volume ↓
- Deliverable: Error message improvements shipped to production

Days 13-14: Analytics Instrumentation

- Task: Implement event tracking for signup, first-call, activation
- Owner: Analytics engineer
- KPI Impact: Enables all future optimization
- Deliverable: Dashboard showing funnel metrics

Exit Criteria:

- ✅ Quickstart completion rate > 70%
- ✅ Median time-to-first-call < 5 minutes
- ✅ All baseline metrics instrumented and visible
- ✅ Zero approval gates between signup and first API call

A.2 Onboarding Optimization Sprint (14 days)

Once foundation is solid, optimize the critical first-impression experience.

Days 1-2: Front Door Usability Test

- Task: Watch 5 developers attempt onboarding with no help
- Owner: DX researcher + Developer advocate
- KPI Impact: Identifies friction points
- Deliverable: Prioritized friction log with severity scores

Days 3-5: Interactive Sandbox

- Task: Build hosted environment where developers can test without setup
- Owner: DevRel engineer
- KPI Impact: Reduces time-to-first-success
- Deliverable: Live sandbox with pre-configured auth

Days 6-8: Sample Application Library

- Task: Create 3 one-click deploy examples (common use cases)
- Owner: Developer advocate + DevRel engineer
- KPI Impact: Activation breadth ↑
- Deliverable: GitHub repo with deploy buttons

Days 9-11: Code Snippet Optimization

- Task: Add copy buttons, language tabs, syntax highlighting
- Owner: Technical writer + Frontend engineer
- KPI Impact: Docs engagement ↑
- Deliverable: Enhanced code blocks across all docs

Days 12-14: Video Walkthrough

- Task: Record 2-minute "Getting Started" video
- Owner: Developer advocate
- KPI Impact: Reduces support load
- Deliverable: Published video linked from docs

Exit Criteria:

- ✅ First-call success rate > 80%
- ✅ Median time-to-first-call < 3 minutes
- ✅ Top 3 friction points from usability test resolved
- ✅ Sandbox usage > 30% of new signups

A.3 Activation Acceleration Sprint (21 days)

Move developers from toy examples to production-ready implementations.

Days 1-3: Reference Architecture

- Task: Document production-ready patterns for top use case
- Owner: Solutions architect + Developer advocate
- KPI Impact: Production adoption ↑
- Deliverable: Architecture blueprint with deployment checklist

Days 4-7: SDK Error Handling

- Task: Add retry helpers and exponential backoff to all SDKs
- Owner: DevRel engineer
- KPI Impact: Error rate ↓
- Deliverable: SDK releases with improved reliability

Days 8-10: Observability Starter Pack

- Task: Create pre-built dashboard templates (Grafana/Datadog)
- Owner: SRE + DevRel engineer
- KPI Impact: Time-to-production-ready ↓
- Deliverable: Public dashboard templates repository

Days 11-14: Integration Guides

- Task: Write guides for top 3 popular frameworks/tools
- Owner: Technical writer
- KPI Impact: Feature breadth ↑
- Deliverable: Published integration documentation

Days 15-18: Production Checklist

- Task: Create go-live checklist covering security, scale, monitoring
- Owner: Security + SRE + Technical writer
- KPI Impact: Production confidence ↑
- Deliverable: Interactive checklist published in docs

Days 19-21: Analytics & Retrospective

- Task: Review activation metrics, identify next bottleneck
- Owner: Analytics engineer + Product manager
- KPI Impact: Informs next sprint
- Deliverable: Activation dashboard and prioritized improvements

Exit Criteria:

- ✅ 7-day activation rate > 20%
- ✅ Production key creation rate increasing
- ✅ All top 3 use cases have reference architectures
- ✅ Error rate for activated users < 2%

A.4 Sprint Execution Best Practices

Daily Standup Pattern:

- Yesterday: What shipped?
- Today: What's blocked?
- Metrics: Are we trending toward exit criteria?
- Duration: 15 minutes maximum

Mid-Sprint Review (Day 7):

- Review metrics against targets
- Adjust priorities if needed
- Communicate blockers to leadership
- Celebrate early wins

Sprint Retrospective (Final day):

- What worked well?
- What slowed us down?
- What should we do differently next sprint?
- Update sprint template based on learnings

Measurement Cadence:

- Track leading indicators daily (task completion, PR merges)
- Review lagging indicators weekly (activation rate, time-to-first-call)
- Report to stakeholders bi-weekly with trend lines

These sprint plans are starting points. Adapt the timeline, owners, and deliverables to match your team size, product complexity, and organizational constraints. The key is maintaining focus on one clear outcome per sprint rather than trying to improve everything simultaneously.

A.5 ICP Builder & Scoring Framework

Choosing the right developer ICP isn't guesswork. This framework helps you systematically evaluate and compare developer segments to identify where to focus your efforts.

Complete ICP canvas template

For each potential developer segment, complete this canvas:

Segment name: Give it a memorable name (e.g., "React Frontend Builders", "Fintech Backend Engineers")

Four-axis definition:

- Technical context: What stack/languages/frameworks do they use?
- Company stage: Startup, growth-stage, or enterprise?
- Team size: Solo developers, small teams (2-5), or large organizations (6+)?
- Use case: What specific problem are they trying to solve?

Anti-persona: Who is NOT in this segment? Be explicit about who you're excluding to maintain focus.

Jobs, pains, and outcomes:

- Jobs to be done: What are they trying to accomplish?
- Current pains: What frustrates them about existing solutions?

- Desired outcomes: What does success look like for them?
- Evidence: What data supports these observations? (interviews, support tickets, usage patterns)

Triggers and timing:

- What event triggers their search for a solution?
- What's their typical evaluation timeline?
- Are there seasonal patterns to their adoption?

Evaluation criteria and deal-breakers:

- What do they evaluate when choosing a platform?
- What are absolute non-starters (e.g., no Python SDK = instant disqualification)?
- What documentation do they read first?

Activation event and target time:

- What specific action indicates real adoption (not just signup)?
- What's the target time from signup to activation?
- Example: "First production API call within 48 hours"

Hello World path:

- Step 1: How do they discover your platform?
- Step 2: What's their first interaction?
- Steps 3-N: What's the critical path to first value?

Top 3 assets to ship next:

- Based on this ICP's needs, what content/tools would accelerate adoption?
- Prioritize based on impact and effort

Integration environment map:

- What tools/platforms do they already use?
- What integrations would make adoption seamless?
- Example: "Typically use: React + Next.js + Vercel + Stripe"

Metrics (leading and lagging) with targets:

- Leading indicators: What predicts this segment's success?
- Lagging indicators: What proves they've activated?
- Specific targets for each metric

Partners and integrations:

- Who serves this segment well?
- What partnership opportunities exist?

ICP fit score:

- Calculate using the scoring worksheet below

Owner and review date:

- Who owns this ICP definition?
- When will you next review and update it?

ICP validation checklist

Don't just guess at your ICP. Validate with real data:

1. Interview 5-10 developers who represent your hypothesis

- Ask about their workflow, pain points, and tool evaluation process
- Test whether your assumptions about their needs are accurate
- Document quotes and insights that validate or challenge your ICP

2. Analyze which users activate fastest and stay longest

- Query your database for patterns in high-value users
- Look for common attributes (company size, tech stack, use case)
- Calculate activation rates by segment

3. Look at support tickets to identify patterns in who struggles

- Which segments generate the most support volume?
- What questions do different segments ask?
- Are there segments that succeed with minimal help?

4. Test content and examples targeted at your ICP and measure engagement

- Create a tutorial specifically for this segment
- Track completion rates and time-on-page

- A/B test ICP-specific messaging vs. generic messaging

5. Refine and iterate quarterly as you learn more

- Review ICP definitions every 90 days
- Update based on new data and market changes
- Archive old ICPs and document what you learned

Scoring worksheet

Use this framework to compare up to three segments and determine which deserves focus.

For each segment, score 1-5 (1=low, 5=high):

Pain (1-5): How acutely does this segment feel the problem you solve?

- 1 = Nice to have
- 3 = Significant pain, but workarounds exist
- 5 = Critical blocker, no good alternatives

Urgency (1-5): How quickly do they need to solve this problem?

- 1 = Someday/maybe
- 3 = This quarter
- 5 = This week

Activation ease today (1-5): Given your current product and docs, how easily can this segment activate?

- 1 = Major gaps, won't succeed
- 3 = Possible but friction-heavy

- 5 = Smooth path to value

Strategic value (1-5): How valuable is this segment long-term?

- 1 = Low monetization potential
- 3 = Good long-term revenue
- 5 = High LTV, network effects, strategic accounts

ICP fit score = (Pain × Urgency × Activation ease × Strategic value) / 100

Higher scores indicate better segment fit. Focus on segments scoring 3.0+.

Segment	Pain	Urgency	Activation Ease	Strategic Value	ICP Fit Score
Segment A	4	5	3	4	2.40
Segment B	5	4	4	5	4.00
Segment C	3	3	5	3	1.35

In this example, Segment B (score: 4.00) should be your primary focus.

Making the decision

Once you've scored segments:

- **If you have 1 person:** Focus exclusively on your highest-scoring segment. Narrow is better than scattered.
- **If you have 2-3 people:** Primary segment gets 70% of effort, secondary gets 30%.

- **If you have 4+ people:** You can serve 2-3 segments, but assign clear ownership and avoid overlap.

Red flags:

- Multiple segments with similar scores → You haven't differentiated enough
- No segment scores above 2.5 → Your product may not have clear PMF yet
- Highest-scoring segment has activation ease = 1 → Fix product before scaling DevRel

This framework prevents the common mistake of trying to serve everyone. By systematically evaluating developer segments, you can focus your limited DevRel resources where they'll have maximum impact.

A.6 Developer Archetypes

Not all developers have the same goals or workflows. Understanding the four primary archetypes helps you create content calendars and programs that serve the full spectrum of your audience.

The four developer archetypes

Archetype	Primary Goal	Preferred Assets	Risk if Ignored
Hacker	Weekend prototypes, rapid experimentation	Quickstarts, code sandboxes, one-click deploy examples	Churns before activation—never gets past Hello World
Integrator	Fit your tool into existing stack seamlessly	Detailed API reference, migration guides, integration tutorials	Abandons during activation when integration is harder than expected
Architect	Long-term reliability, scale, security	SLAs, security whitepapers, IAM documentation, architecture diagrams	Blocks enterprise deals—can't get buy-in without compliance docs
Evangelist	Thought leadership, community visibility	Community speaking slots, case study collaborations, co-marketing opportunities	Influences peers toward competitors—missed advocacy multiplication

How to apply developer archetypes

Content calendar balance

A healthy DevRel content calendar addresses all four archetypes each quarter. Don't over-index on Hackers (Quickstarts only) while ignoring Architects (enterprise security).

The most effective approach is to audit your content quarterly and ensure you have at least one substantial piece of content for each archetype. This doesn't mean equal distribution, your ICP might skew toward certain archetypes, but complete neglect of any archetype creates blind spots.

Funnel stage mapping

Different archetypes dominate different stages of the developer journey:

- **Awareness → Hacker & Evangelist:** Quick demos and community visibility attract these developers first. Hackers want to see "can I build something cool in 10 minutes?" Evangelists want to see "is this worth talking about?"

- **Onboarding → Hacker:** Fast path to first success is critical. Hackers will abandon if they can't get something working quickly. Your quickstart is primarily for this archetype.

- **Activation → Integrator:** Seamless integration into existing workflows determines whether developers move to production. Integrators need detailed guides showing how your platform fits their stack.

- **Engagement → Evangelist:** Community programs, speaking opportunities, and co-marketing appeal most to Evangelists. They want to build their reputation and share knowledge.

- **Monetization → Architect:** Enterprise features, compliance documentation, and SLAs matter most to Architects evaluating long-term commitment and cost.

Warning signs of neglect

Pay attention to these patterns that indicate you're over-serving one archetype while neglecting others:

- **Too Hacker-focused:** High signup conversion but low production adoption. Lots of developers try your platform but few deploy to production. You're great at quick demos but haven't helped developers integrate into real workflows.

- **Too Integrator-focused:** Great docs but low awareness. Your existing users love the detailed documentation, but new developers aren't discovering you. You've optimized for depth without investing in top-of-funnel.

- **Too Architect-focused:** Enterprise success but individual developers struggle. You win large contracts but individual developers find your platform too complex or heavyweight for their needs. This can limit bottom-up adoption.

- **Too Evangelist-focused:** Lots of buzz but low actual usage. High social media engagement and conference presence, but metrics show limited real adoption. You're generating interest without converting it to activation.

Quarterly content audit

Every 90 days, review your content output and ask:

1. Have we shipped something meaningful for each archetype this quarter?
2. Which archetype is over-represented in our content?
3. Which archetype are we neglecting?
4. Does our content distribution align with our ICP's archetype profile?

If you haven't shipped something for each archetype in the past 90 days, you have a gap. This doesn't mean you need perfect balance, if your ICP is primarily Integrators, you should skew toward integration content. But complete neglect of any archetype creates vulnerabilities.

Connecting archetypes to ICP

When you define your ICP (see A.5), consider which archetypes best describe your target developers:

- A startup founder exploring new tools → Hacker tendencies
- A senior engineer evaluating platforms for production → Integrator + Architect
- A developer advocate at a company → Evangelist
- A CTO making strategic decisions → Architect

Understanding your ICP's archetype profile helps you prioritize content and programs. If your ICP is 60% Integrator, 30% Architect, 10% Hacker, your content calendar should roughly reflect those proportions, with the caveat that you still need some content for all archetypes to serve the full developer journey.

Practical application example

Let's say you're building a payment API and your ICP is e-commerce engineering teams at growth-stage startups. Here's how you might apply archetypes:

Hacker content (20% of calendar):

- "Accept your first payment in 5 minutes" quickstart
- Interactive payment form builder
- One-click deploy Shopify integration

Integrator content (40% of calendar):

- Next.js integration guide
- Migration guide from Stripe
- Webhook handling best practices
- Error handling patterns

Architect content (30% of calendar):

- PCI compliance whitepaper
- Security architecture deep dive
- Scaling to 10,000 transactions/second
- Disaster recovery playbook

Evangelist content (10% of calendar):

- Case study co-marketing with successful customers
- Speaking slots at fintech meetups
- Guest posts on e-commerce blogs
- Community showcase program

This distribution reflects that your ICP needs deep integration guidance and enterprise-grade reliability, while still serving developers who want to experiment quickly and those who want to build their reputation.

Key takeaway

Developer archetypes provide a framework for ensuring your DevRel programs serve the complete spectrum of developer needs. Use them alongside your ICP definition (A.5) to create balanced content calendars and identify gaps in your developer experience.

B. Interview Formats

Effective user interviews uncover insights that metrics alone cannot reveal.

Discovery interview structure

Warm-up (5 minutes): Build rapport, explain purpose, assure confidentiality

Background (10 minutes): Understand their role, tech stack, current tools

Problem exploration (20 minutes): Dig into pain points, workflows, and challenges

Solution evaluation (15 minutes): If they've used your product, understand their experience

Future needs (10 minutes): What would make them more successful?

Key techniques:

- Ask "why" repeatedly to uncover root causes
- Focus on specific examples rather than generalities
- Stay curious and avoid leading questions
- Record with permission for later analysis

Sample questions to ask

Discovery interviews:

- "Walk me through the last time you integrated a new API. What went well? What was frustrating?"
- "What would have made you give up on our platform in the first 24 hours?"
- "Show me your current workflow. Where does [our product] fit in?"
- "What's the worst error message you've encountered recently, and why was it bad?"
- "If you could change one thing about our documentation, what would it be?"

Beta program interviews:

- "What surprised you most when using this feature?"
- "If you were documenting this for a colleague, what would you warn them about?"
- "What almost made you stop testing?"
- "Which part of the feature did you understand immediately, and which confused you?"

Churned user interviews:

- "What was the moment you decided to stop using our platform?"
- "What could we have done differently to keep you?"
- "What are you using instead, and why is it better?"
- "Looking back, what was the first sign things weren't working?"

Beta program interview structure

For beta participants, focus on feedback that improves the product:

- What worked well? Identify strengths to preserve
- What was confusing? Surface documentation gaps
- What broke? Find bugs and edge cases
- What's missing? Discover feature gaps
- Would you recommend this? Gauge satisfaction and reasons

Synthesizing findings

After 5-10 interviews, look for patterns: Are 3+ people hitting the same friction point? Document exact quotes with context. Prioritize based on: (1) frequency mentioned, (2) severity of impact, (3) effort to fix. Create one-pagers per theme with **problem → representative quotes → recommended action → estimated impact**. Share these with product teams within 48 hours while insights are fresh.

Interview best practices

- **Conduct 5-10 interviews per research question** (diminishing returns after 10)
- **Offer small incentives:** $50 gift card, exclusive swag, early feature access
- **Record with permission,** take notes on key quotes and body language
- **Avoid leading questions:** Don't say "Don't you think X is confusing?" Instead ask "What confused you?"
- **Schedule 30-45 minutes:** Enough depth without fatigue
- **Interview within 7 days of key events:** Churn decision, beta completion, first activation

C. Presentation Skills for Advocates

Public speaking is a core DevRel skill. Here are battle-tested techniques:

Demo preparation checklist

- Test demo 3 times before the presentation
- Have offline backup of everything
- Prepare for failure scenarios
- Reset demo environment between runs
- Close unnecessary apps and notifications
- Increase font sizes for visibility

Talk structure that works

Hook (2 minutes): Compelling problem or surprising insight

Context (3 minutes): Why this matters, who it's for

Core content (15 minutes): 3-5 key points maximum

Demo/example (10 minutes): Show, don't just tell

Conclusion (5 minutes): Recap, call to action, resources

Handling Q&A

- Repeat questions so everyone hears them
- "I don't know, but I'll find out" is a perfectly acceptable answer
- Bridge to your key points when possible
- Keep answers concise to allow more questions
- Collect contact information for detailed follow-ups

D. Tools We Love

Community platforms

- **Discord:** Best for real-time developer communities
- **Discourse:** Excellent for searchable, long-form discussions
- **Slack (via Slack Connect):** Good for customer communities
- **GitHub Discussions:** Perfect for open-source projects

Analytics and metrics

- **PostHog:** Product analytics with session recording
- **Mixpanel/Amplitude:** User behavior tracking
- **Metabase:** Self-service business intelligence
- **Orbit:** Community relationship management

Content creation

- **Loom:** Quick video tutorials
- **Notion/GitBook:** Documentation platforms
- **Snagit/CleanShot:** Screenshot and annotation
- **Carbon:** Beautiful code screenshots

Developer tools

- **httpie:** User-friendly HTTP client
- **Postman:** API testing and documentation
- **ngrok:** Expose local dev servers
- **jq:** JSON processor for CLI

E. Sample AI Prompts for Scaling DevRel

Generative AI can accelerate DevRel workflows when used thoughtfully. These prompts provide starting points for common tasks, but always verify outputs for accuracy and brand voice.

Content creation prompts

Generate tutorial outlines:

Create a tutorial outline for [task] using [product/API]. Include: prerequisites, step-by-step instructions, code examples, common errors, and next steps.

Improve error messages:

Here's our current error message: [message]. Rewrite it to be more helpful by: 1) Explaining what went wrong, 2) Why it might have happened, 3) How to fix it, 4) Where to get more help.

Create FAQ answers:

Based on these support tickets [paste tickets], generate FAQ entries in this format: Question, Quick answer (2 sentences), Detailed explanation, Related resources.

Summarize community discussions:

Summarize this Discord/forum thread [paste content] into: Key question, Main discussion points, Consensus/resolution, Action items.

Code and SDK prompts

Generate multi-language code examples:

Convert this [language] code example to [target languages]. Maintain the same logic and comments. Code: [paste code]

Target languages: Python, JavaScript, Ruby, Go

Ensure idiomatic patterns for each language.

Create SDK usage examples:

Generate a working code example showing how to [specific task] using our [SDK name] SDK in [language]. Include: import statements, authentication, error handling, expected output.

Documentation automation

Convert commits to release notes:

Transform these git commits into user-facing release notes. Group by: New Features, Improvements, Bug Fixes, Breaking Changes.

Commits: [paste commits]

Use friendly language, not technical jargon. Focus on user impact.

Generate troubleshooting guides:

Based on these error patterns and solutions [paste support data], create a troubleshooting guide with: Problem symptoms, Likely causes, Step-by-step solutions, Prevention tips.

Content adaptation

Adapt content for skill levels:

Rewrite this technical content for [beginner/intermediate/advanced] developers:

[paste content]

Beginner: Use analogies, avoid jargon, explain concepts step-by-step

Intermediate: Assume basic knowledge, focus on practical application

Advanced: Technical depth, edge cases, performance considerations

Convert documentation formats:

Convert this documentation into a [video script/blog post/social media thread]:

[paste documentation]

Maintain key technical points but adapt tone and structure for [target format].

Quality control checklist

Before publishing AI-generated content:

- **Verify technical accuracy:** Test all code examples, confirm API endpoints exist
- **Check for hallucinations:** Cross-reference claims against official documentation

- **Match brand voice:** Edit for consistent tone and terminology
- **Review for bias:** Ensure inclusive language and diverse examples
- **Update timestamps:** Add "Last verified: [date]" to prevent stale information

When NOT to use AI

Avoid AI for:

- **Security-sensitive content:** Authentication flows, encryption implementations, security advisories
- **Legally binding text:** Terms of service, privacy policies, SLAs, compliance documentation
- **Crisis communications:** Breaking changes, outages, security incidents require human judgment
- **Architectural decisions:** AI cannot weigh your specific technical constraints and business context
- **Personal user communications:** Support tickets, community moderation, direct feedback require human empathy

Use AI to accelerate, not replace, human expertise and judgment.

F. Quick Reference Tables

Metric benchmarks by stage

Stage	Metric	Good	Great	Excellent
Awareness	Docs→ Quick start CTR	0.7%	1.0%	1.5%+
Onboarding	Completion rate	40%	60%	80%+
Activation	24h activation	15%	25%	35%+
Engagement	Answer rate < 24h	50%	65%	80%+
Monetization	Trial→ Paid	8%	12%	18%+

DevRel headcount by company stage

Stage	Monthly Signups	Suggested DevRel Team
Early	< 100	1 generalist
Growth	100-500	2-3 (content + community)
Scale	500-2000	4-6 (specialized roles)
Enterprise	2000+	7+ (full functional team)

Content production schedule

Content Type	Frequency	Owner	Distribution
API changelog	Weekly	Product	Email, RSS
Tutorial	Biweekly	DevRel	Blog, SEO
Video	Monthly	DevRel	YouTube, social
Webinar	Quarterly	DevRel	Registration, recording
Conference talk	2-4/year	Advocates	Conference, blog

G. Quick Wins & 90-Day Roadmaps

This section provides actionable playbooks for teams that need to show progress quickly while building toward long-term success.

Quick wins to tackle this week

These are high-impact, low-effort activities you can complete in the next 5 business days. Each is designed to deliver immediate value while requiring minimal coordination.

Priority	Action	Effort	Impact	Owner
1	Ship 5-minute Quickstart with copy-paste code	4 hours	High (activation)	Developer advocate
2	Embed basic analytics (PostHog/Mixpanel) on docs	2 hours	Medium (insights)	DevRel engineer
3	Create #friction-log Slack channel with Eng+PM	1 hour	High (feedback loop)	Community manager
4	Draft deprecation policy for APIs (12-month sunset)	3 hours	Medium (trust)	API product manager
5	Announce monthly community showcase in newsletter	2 hours	Medium (recognition)	Community manager

Implementation notes:

- Prioritize tasks 1-3 if you lack activation data
- Tasks 4-5 build long-term trust and engagement
- All tasks should be completable by a single person or pair
- Schedule a Friday demo to celebrate completed wins

30-Day foundation roadmap

Week 1: Baseline & Quick Wins

- Day 1-2: Implement event tracking for signup, first-call, activation
- Day 3-4: Ship Quickstart with embedded analytics
- Day 5: Run first "Front Door" usability test with 3 developers

Week 2: Documentation Sprint

- Day 6-8: Fix top 3 friction points identified in usability tests
- Day 9-10: Add copy buttons, syntax highlighting to code examples
- Day 11-12: Create error message improvement backlog with engineering

Week 3: Community Foundation

- Day 13-15: Set up community platform (Discord/Discourse) with clear guidelines
- Day 16-17: Launch weekly office hours (advertise 2 weeks in advance)
- Day 18-19: Identify and invite 5-10 power users to beta champion program

Week 4: Measurement & Iteration

- Day 20-22: Build first dashboard with activation funnel
- Day 23-24: Run friction log review with product and engineering
- Day 25-27: Present first DevRel metrics review to leadership
- Day 28-30: Plan next 30 days based on what you learned

Success criteria:

- ✅ Time-to-first-call baseline established
- ✅ First usability test completed with documented findings
- ✅ Community platform live with first 50 members
- ✅ Dashboard showing weekly signup and activation trends

90-Day growth roadmap

Days 1-30: Foundation (see 30-day roadmap above)

Days 31-60: Activation & Content

- Week 5-6: Launch SDK improvements based on friction logs
- Week 7: Create 3 use-case-specific tutorials (not just API reference)
- Week 8: Pilot automated changelog and release notes process

Metrics to watch:

- Activation rate trending up 5+ percentage points
- Support ticket volume per new user decreasing
- Documentation engagement (time on page, scroll depth) improving

Days 61-90: Scale & Advocacy

- Week 9: Launch champion/ambassador program with 10-15 participants

- Week 10: Publish first community-contributed tutorial or integration
- Week 11: Pilot developer NPS survey to establish baseline satisfaction
- Week 12: Host first community-led webinar or workshop

Metrics to watch:

- Community answer rate > 50% (peers helping peers)
- Champion program participants contributing content
- NPS score establishes baseline for future measurement

Exit criteria for 90 days:

- ✅ Activation rate improved by 10+ percentage points from baseline
- ✅ Community answering >50% of questions without team intervention
- ✅ At least 2 community members contributing content monthly
- ✅ DevRel metrics presented in quarterly business review
- ✅ Product team prioritizing 2+ items from friction log each sprint

90-Day justification roadmap

For teams that need to justify DevRel investment or secure additional headcount, this roadmap focuses on demonstrating measurable business impact.

Days 1-30: Data Collection & Baselines

- Week 1: Instrument complete funnel (awareness → activation → revenue)
- Week 2: Interview 10 recent signups about their experience
- Week 3: Establish baseline metrics (activation rate, time-to-first-call, support tickets)
- Week 4: Create DevRel attribution model (developer-influenced deals)

Days 31-60: Prove Impact

- Week 5-6: Ship improvements that move 1-2 key metrics
- Week 7: Document cost savings (support deflection, sales engineering time)
- Week 8: Calculate developer lifetime value (DLV) for activated cohorts

Days 61-90: Build the Business Case

- Week 9: Create executive presentation linking DevRel to revenue
- Week 10: Gather testimonials from sales on developer-influenced deals
- Week 11: Model ROI scenarios for expanding the team
- Week 12: Present business case with data to leadership

Artifacts to create:

- One-pager: "DevRel Impact at a Glance" (metrics dashboard screenshot + 3 key wins)
- Business case: "The ROI of Developer Relations" (current state, proposed investment, expected outcomes)
- Stakeholder map: Who supports DevRel? Who needs more convincing? What data would convince them?

Adapting roadmaps to your context

For startups (< 50 employees):

- Focus on 30-day foundation roadmap
- Skip formal champion programs initially
- Prioritize activation over awareness
- Keep metrics simple (3-5 core metrics maximum)

For growth-stage companies (50-500 employees):

- Execute full 90-day growth roadmap
- Invest in measurement infrastructure early
- Build cross-functional alignment rituals
- Pilot champion program with 10-15 participants

For enterprises (500+ employees):

- Extend to 120-day roadmap with dedicated scaling phase
- Emphasize cross-functional collaboration and executive sponsorship
- Build comprehensive attribution models
- Plan for multiple DevRel roles and specialization

For teams under pressure to justify their existence:

- Follow 90-day justification roadmap
- Over-communicate wins to stakeholders weekly
- Tie every activity to business metrics
- Build executive sponsors who understand developer-led growth

The key to any roadmap is measurement and iteration. Set clear exit criteria, review progress weekly, and adjust based on what you learn. Perfect execution of the wrong plan is worse than imperfect execution of the right one.

H. The DevRel Toolchain

Tools are leverage, not strategy. Choose them to shorten feedback loops and reduce cognitive load for both developers and DevRel staff. This section provides a layered architecture you can mix and match based on your needs.

Documentation and content layer

Category	Purpose	Popular Options	Selection Tip
Static site generators	Fast, versioned docs with PR workflow	Docusaurus, Astro, Hugo, MkDocs	Pick one that matches your stack language for easier contributor ramp-up
Headless CMS	Non-dev content edits, scheduled publishing	Sanity, Strapi, Contentful	Ensure Markdown + MDX support to embed live code
Interactive docs	In-browser sandbox, API explorers	ReadMe, Stoplight Elements, Postman Flows	Prioritize tools that log usage analytics for funnel tracking

Key considerations:

- Version control integration for documentation as code
- Search functionality with analytics
- Support for multiple programming languages with tabs
- Mobile responsiveness for developers coding on tablets

Community and communication layer

Purpose	Synchronous	Asynchronous	Searchable Archive
Real-time Q&A	Discord, Slack	---	Use Khoros or ThreadBot to snapshot solved threads into docs
Long-form discussion	---	Discourse, GitHub Discussions	Yes; threads become SEO fuel
Broadcast	Twitter/X, LinkedIn	Monthly newsletter via ConvertKit or Ghost	Archive newsletters in a /changelog feed for discoverability
Live events	Hopin, Bevy, StreamYard	---	Auto-publish recordings to YouTube with chapter markers

Best practices:

- Integrate community platforms with your documentation
- Set up autoresponders for common questions
- Create escalation paths from community to support
- Establish clear community guidelines and moderation policies

Observability and analytics layer

Product telemetry:

- PostHog, Amplitude, Mixpanel to track first-call success, error codes, and latency outliers
- Segment for unified event collection across platforms

Docs analytics:

- Plausible or Google Analytics to track bounce rate and scroll depth
- Tie document slugs to activation events to understand content effectiveness

Community health:

- Orbit, Common Room, or open-source Orbit-Lite dashboards
- Watch newcomer-to-contributor conversion rates
- Track answer rates and response times

Pro tip: Pipe all events into a data warehouse (BigQuery, Snowflake). A single source of truth prevents "dueling dashboards."

Automation and CI/CD layer

Workflow	Tooling	Win
Preview docs per pull request	GitHub Actions + Vercel preview URLs	Contributors see rendered docs before merge
Automatic SDK generation	OpenAPI → liblab, Speakeasy, Fern	Keep SDKs in sync with API changes; reduce manual toil
ChatOps release notes	GitHub Release Drafter + Slack Bot	Ship notes instantly, keeps internal teams aligned
Usage-based billing alerts	Stripe metered billing + Zapier → Slack	Notify DevRel when top accounts near paywall, perfect churn-prevention touchpoint

Infrastructure as code:

- Use Terraform or Pulumi to manage DevRel infrastructure
- Version control all automation scripts
- Document runbooks for common operational tasks

Experimentation and feedback layer

A/B testing:

- LaunchDarkly or GrowthBook for feature flags tied to DX metrics
- Test documentation approaches, onboarding flows, and UI changes

User surveys:

- Typeform or Formbricks

- Trigger surveys after the first three API calls to capture fresh impressions

Session replays:

- FullStory or OpenReplay to watch onboarding friction in real time
- Privacy-first alternatives: PostHog with session recording

Tool evaluation checklist

Before committing to any new tool, ask these questions:

1. **Does it integrate with your auth provider?** SSO fatigue kills adoption. Tools should support your existing identity system.

2. **Can non-developers contribute?** Content only scales if product managers and marketers can edit. Tools requiring engineering expertise for every update create bottlenecks.

3. **Is there an export/migration path?** Avoid vendor lock-in, especially for community data and content. Always have a backup plan.

4. **Does cost scale with value?** Watch for MAU-based pricing hidden in Discord bots or analytics tools. Costs should align with the value delivered.

5. **What's the learning curve?** Every new tool adds cognitive overhead. Prefer tools your team already

knows or that have extensive documentation and community support.

Rule of thumb: Adopt the fewest tools that cover 80% of your workflows. Each new tool adds overhead. Plan quarterly tooling audits to sunset underutilized platforms.

Sample toolchain configurations

Startup (1-2 person DevRel team):

- Docs: Docusaurus + GitHub Pages
- Community: Discord + GitHub Discussions
- Analytics: PostHog (free tier)
- Automation: GitHub Actions only
- **Total monthly cost:** < $100

Growth stage (3-5 person team):

- Docs: ReadMe or GitBook
- Community: Discord + Discourse
- Analytics: Amplitude + Orbit
- Automation: GitHub Actions + Zapier
- CI/CD: Vercel + automated SDK generation
- **Total monthly cost:** $500-1500

Enterprise (6+ person team):

- Docs: Custom headless CMS + Docusaurus
- Community: Slack Connect + Discourse + Khoros
- Analytics: Snowflake data warehouse + Looker
- Automation: Full CI/CD pipeline + custom tooling

- Developer portal: Custom-built on your platform
- **Total monthly cost:** $5000-15000+

Remember: start minimal and add tools only when you feel the pain of not having them. The best toolchain is the one your team actually uses.

I. Instrumentation Framework

Great metrics start with excellent plumbing. If your pipes leak, your dashboard lies. Instrumentation is the invisible backbone of every data-driven DevRel program. Without it, you're guessing. With it, you can draw a straight line from tutorial tweaks to revenue growth.

The three-layer stack

1. Event capture (What happened?)

Client SDKs, server middleware, or API gateway logs emit raw events. Use libraries that batch and retry to avoid slowing the user path.

Key implementation details:

- Event naming convention: noun_verb format (e.g., quickstart_completed, api_call_production)
- Required fields: user_id, timestamp, event_name, session_id
- Optional but valuable: environment (sandbox/production), sdk_version, language, framework

2. Transformation and storage (How do we clean and enrich?)

ETL/ELT tools (dbt, Airbyte) deduplicate, add context (environment, plan, language), and load into a warehouse.

Best practices:

- Data contracts guarantee every event has required fields
- Use JSON schemas or TypeScript types for validation
- Deduplicate using deterministic keys (event_id, user_id, timestamp)
- Enrich with user metadata (signup date, plan tier, company size)

3. Visualization and alerting (Who needs to know and when?)

Dashboards in Looker, Metabase, or PostHog turn events into funnels. Slack alerts fire when metrics cross "red-zone" thresholds.

Rule of thumb: One source of truth (warehouse), one model of truth (dbt), many views of truth (dashboards).

Choosing tools wisely

Start with managed services: Segment, PostHog Cloud, or Supabase logs until you prove ROI. Don't build custom infrastructure until you have clear requirements based on actual usage.

Prioritize SDK availability: If half your users code in Go, choose an event pipeline with a solid Go client. Missing SDK support creates instrumentation gaps.

Avoid vendor lock-in traps: Store raw events in your warehouse, not just in the SaaS UI. This enables switching analytics tools without losing historical data.

Data quality best practices

Schema registry:

- Document every event in a versioned repository
- PR changes like you do code
- Include example payloads and field descriptions
- Version events when schemas change (quickstart_completed_v2)

Required properties:

- Enforce with runtime validation (JSON Schema or TypeScript types)
- Fail fast when required fields are missing
- Log validation errors for debugging

Idempotency:

- Use deterministic dedupe keys (event_id, user_id, timestamp)
- Prevents double-counting when events are retried
- Essential for accurate conversion metrics

Sampling:

- Never sample activation events
- Sample high-volume /healthcheck pings instead

- Use consistent hashing so same user always sampled or not

Privacy and compliance

Data minimization:

- Hash or tokenize personal data before it leaves the client
- Don't log email addresses in events unless absolutely necessary
- Store PII in separate, secured schemas

User consent:

- Follow GDPR/CCPA opt-out flags in your SDKs
- Implement right-to-be-forgotten workflows
- Document data retention policies

Access controls:

- Limit who can query raw event data
- Use role-based access for analytics tools
- Audit access to PII regularly

90-Day implementation roadmap

Weeks 1-2: Define and instrument

- Define activation event schema
- Set up Segment/PostHog in staging environment
- Instrument Quickstart completion tracking

Weeks 3-4: Core events

- Instrument API gateway for first-call tracking
- Add SDK download/initialization events
- Deploy to production with monitoring

Weeks 5-6: Data modeling

- Ship dbt models for TTFA (time to first activation)
- Create activation rate calculations
- Set up data quality checks

Weeks 7-8: Dashboards

- Build Looker/Metabase dashboard with core metrics
- Share read-only links with product and executives
- Gather feedback on missing metrics

Weeks 9-12: Alerts and iteration

- Add Slack alerts for critical threshold breaches
- Run first metric review with stakeholders
- Open backlog tickets for identified data gaps
- Document instrumentation patterns for future events

Pro tip: Track these metrics before anything else: docs → Quickstart CTR, Quickstart completion rate, TTFA, 401/403 error rate, 7-day retention.

Anti-patterns to avoid

"Log everything" syndrome: More events ≠ more insight. Each event should answer a specific decision-making question. Random instrumentation creates noise.

Dashboard hoarding: Ten dashboards nobody checks is worse than one everyone trusts. Consolidate to 1-2 primary dashboards.

Event drift: Developers rename fields without updating downstream models. Adopt CI tests on event schemas to catch breaking changes.

Delayed ETL: If data lands the next day, your alerts arrive too late. Aim for < 15 minute latency on activation events.

Missing business context: Events without user metadata (plan tier, company size, signup date) limit analysis. Enrich early in the pipeline.

Sample event schemas

Quickstart completion:

{

"event": "quickstart_completed",

"user_id": "usr_abc123",

"timestamp": "2026-01-19T14:30:00Z",

"session_id": "ses_xyz789",

"quickstart_id": "getting-started",

"language": "python",

"time_spent_seconds": 180,

"environment": "sandbox"

}

First API call:

{

"event": "api_call_first",

"user_id": "usr_abc123",

"timestamp": "2026-01-19T14:35:00Z",

"endpoint": "/v1/messages",

"method": "POST",

"status_code": 200,

"response_time_ms": 145,

"sdk_version": "python-2.1.0",

"environment": "sandbox"

}

Production activation:

{

"event": "api_call_production",

"user_id": "usr_abc123",

"timestamp": "2026-01-20T09:15:00Z",

"endpoint": "/v1/messages",

"method": "POST",

"status_code": 201,

"environment": "production",

"days_since_signup": 1

}

Key metric calculations

Time to First Activation (TTFA):

```
SELECT

PERCENTILE_CONT(0.5) WITHIN GROUP (ORDER BY seconds_to_first_call) as median_ttfa

FROM (

SELECT
```

user_id,

EXTRACT(EPOCH FROM (first_call_at - signup_at)) as seconds_to_first_call

FROM users

WHERE first_call_at IS NOT NULL

)

7-Day Activation Rate:

SELECT

COUNT(DISTINCT CASE WHEN activated THEN user_id END) * 100.0 / COUNT(DISTINCT user_id) as activation_rate

FROM (

SELECT

u.user_id,

CASE WHEN pc.user_id IS NOT NULL THEN TRUE ELSE FALSE END as activated

FROM users u

LEFT JOIN (

SELECT DISTINCT user_id

FROM events

WHERE event = 'api_call_production'

AND timestamp <= u.signup_at + INTERVAL '7 days'

) pc ON u.user_id = pc.user_id

WHERE u.signup_at >= CURRENT_DATE - INTERVAL '30 days'

)

Bottom line: Instrumentation isn't glamorous, but it's the leverage that turns DevRel anecdotes into product truth.

Made in the USA
Monee, IL
04 November 2026

67384070R00134